ESSENTIALS NEGOTIATION

ESSENTIALS

NEGOTIATION

KATIA TIELEMAN &
MARC BUELENS

LANNOO CAMPUS

Second edition: August 2013

Publishing house LannooCampus
Erasme Ruelensvest 179 bus 101
B-3001 Leuven (Belgium)
www.lannoocampus.com

Design: Wendy De Haes

D/2012/45/567 – isbn 978 94 014 0295 8 – nur 801, 806

CONTENTS

INTRODUCTION

NEGOTIATING – EVERYONE IS DOING IT!

In a world where politics seemingly equals bickering, where corporate mergers break or are broken and where collective bargaining is like a public game of chess, we have all become familiar with the concept of negotiation. Not a day passes without some form of negotiation making headlines.

But negotiation affects people in many more than these most obvious ways. The tug-of-war that takes place in the political and business arenas is just the tip of the iceberg. Whether we realize it or not, we constantly engage in negotiation, each and every day. We negotiate about next year's holiday destination. We negotiate about whether the kids can stay up late on Friday night, who will put the rubbish out and who will get first go in the shower tomorrow morning. In meetings at work we negotiate about the way you want a specific project to be carried out, about risks to be taken, tasks to be allocated, even about promotions and pay. At a higher level, we negotiate about strategic development and budgetary decisions.

In essence, negotiation is nothing more and nothing less than a process of interaction for solving problems, making common decisions and, above all, creating opportunities. As such, everyone is a negotiator and, perhaps surprisingly, many of the mechanisms involved in top level negotiation are fundamentally the same as the mechanisms behind negotiating your next salary increase with your boss or discussing a whole range of other matters with your colleagues, partners and children. For this reason it is vital that you understand and are able to manage the mechanisms on which negotiation is based, so that you can realize your full negotiation potential. This book will help you to do precisely that.

Smart negotiation is important not only because we all negotiate, but also because we need to do it more and more. Research has shown that managers spend more than one third of their time either directly or indirectly engaged in the processes of negotiation or conflict resolution.[1] We must (and may!) negotiate ever more often.

One of the reasons for this is that traditional patterns of authority and hierarchy are rapidly disappearing. As a result, today's managers and leaders are becoming bridge-builders, far more so than the experts or bosses they would have been just a few decades ago. One of their key qualities is that they can lead people towards a consensus. Generation Y is not prepared to participate just because someone in authority tells them to. They need to be convinced of a project or an idea.[2] Managers and leaders can rely less and less on plain formal authority. They have become negotiating managers, more concerned than ever before with innovation, staff motivation, process management and the reconciliation of differing opinions. At the same time, the opinions of an increasing number of stakeholders need to be taken into account. We are evolving from shareholder capitalism to stakeholder capitalism, in which the main task of the manager is negotiation within the context of multi-stakeholder management. In today's knowledge economy the success of a company is in good part determined by its network of collaborative partners (see also Chapter 5). And again, these rules apply well beyond the corporate management that we use as the most obvious example here. Also as an employee, entrepreneur, parent or relational partner "you don't necessarily get what you deserve, but what you negotiate."[3] We must – and should! – negotiate more.

In fact, historically, we can speak of a maturity continuum with regard to our method of collaborating with each other: from dependence to independence and finally to mutual dependence or interdependence. In dependence thinking the focus is external: 'You must take care of me – I am dependent on you'. In independence thinking the focus is internal: 'I can do this alone, I don't need anyone, I will do it my way. My actions will be dictated neither by tradition nor by anyone else!' In interdependence thinking the focus is on interaction and collaboration: 'We can work together. We can combine our talents and opportunities.' In interdependence thinking, the whole is greater than the sum of its parts. It allows us to increase the size of the cake to be shared among the partners.

Yet, while our environment increasingly demands collaborative thinking, our own convictions and negotiating paradigm are typically still on a very different wavelength.

ARE WE DOOMED TO FIGHT?

The world in which we negotiate is hard. It is a world of eat or be eaten. Essentially, we are killer apes – conflict and aggression are built into our genes as an evolutionary survival strategy. The 'win-win' argument sounds good in theory, but in practice we are guided by the survival of the fittest. All that protects us as a society from the dictatorship of the strongest is a thin veneer of culture and civilization, right?

The roots of modern biology and our modern industrial system are closely intertwined. Darwin's discoveries in the 19th century went hand in hand with the development of industrial capitalism. From these intertwined developments, Social Darwinism emerged, which views life as a battle 'in which those who make it should not let themselves be dragged down by those who don't.'[4]

Herbert Spencer translated what he saw as the "natural laws" of the right of the strongest into economic and business terminology. Huge numbers of his books were sold[5] and the great industrialists of the day were quick to adopt his language: "While the law [of competition] may sometimes be hard for the individual, it is the best for the race, because it ensures the survival of the fittest in every department."[6] Philosophers also embraced the message: "If evolution and the survival of the fittest be true at all, the destruction of prey and of human rivals must have been among the most important. [...] It is just because human bloodthirstiness is such a primitive part of us that it is so hard to eradicate, especially when a fight or a hunt is promised as part of the fun" (James, 1890).[7]

Already in *Il Principe* (*The Prince*, 1532), the famous book written for the Italian Medici family, Machiavelli had explained to would-be rulers that it is better to be feared than to be loved and that lying is an indispensable weapon in the labyrinthine world of diplomatic intrigue.[8] In the social sciences, just over a century later Thomas Hobbes argued that man was a wolf towards other men (*homo homini lupus*). Intertwining the roots of our current economic system with biological discoveries finds legitimacy with the architects of modern diplomacy, while at the same time turning the ideas of into clichés.

Within this cultural, philosophical, scientific and economic context, a negotiating paradigm gradually developed of a competitive, 'every-man-for-himself', conflict-oriented society. Competition became a natural law, a slogan for the business world that soon came to dominate economic thinking. Implicitly or explicitly, it is still the paradigm that most managers use when negotiating today. 'Collaboration and trust' sound great, but are just a bit too naïve.

It should come as no surprise that this attitude is not conducive to fruitful negotiation. Indeed, the figures speak for themselves.

In a US survey, some 85% of all employees confirmed that they were regularly confronted with escalating conflicts in the work place. Asked how these manifested themselves and what the consequences were, 27% answered that the conflicts involved personal insults and attacks.

Of these, one quarter resulted in health problems and absence. Conflicts ranged from bullying (18%) to conflicts among departments (18%). Another 18% mentioned that people regularly leave the organization as a result of conflict, whereas 16% mentioned dismissal and 13% referred to transfers to other departments. Some believed that the inability to manage conflict was a major reason for project failure (9%). Others admitted to avoiding certain colleagues because of differences of opinion (67%). One in four said that they had called in sick to temporarily escape a conflict situation.

The expense to the economy is huge. In 2008, estimations of lost working time due to conflicts in just the United States reached a staggering 359 billion dollars.[9] Even so, 70% of employees see conflict management and negotiation as critical leadership skills. For 34% of staff and 19% of managers the atmosphere in the work place is the most important factor affecting motivation. This made it the most important determinant for staff and the second most important determinant for managers (after the level of salary).[10] The legal costs of conflicts (including conflicts between companies) were assessed to amount to 5% of gross company income in 2005. They have continued to rise since then.[11]

Are we doomed to incur these high financial and relational costs? Is there nothing we can do?

A NEW NEGOTIATING PARADIGM

The previous section explained that our current view and practice of negotiation originates and finds legitimacy in the way we see human nature from a biological point of view. But is this view correct? Does the shadow of Machiavelli still stalk every negotiating table? And if so, is this a good thing? Were thinkers like Darwin, Spencer and Hobbes – as founders of the way we think about human interaction and human nature – actually right? Or have we interpreted their conclusions too literally and perhaps bent them slightly to justify existing practice?

Two male apes have just had a fight. It is perfectly possible for them to keep out of each other's way. There is plenty of space. But what do they do? They go and sit next to each other. They don't dare look at each other, but they gradually edge closer and closer. However, before they touch an older female intervenes and tends the wounds of one of the males. When she moves to do the same for the other male, the first one follows her example. (If the first male fails to follow voluntarily, the other apes, particularly the females, will encourage him to do so.) In this way, the second male eventually receives the same care and attention. After a time, the female leaves the two males alone. And what happens now? The two 'enemies' of just a few minutes ago now tend each other's wounds. (From Frans de Waal (2009), biologist, psychologist and one of the world's leading primate experts.)

The current debate in biological circles is characterized by a plea from leading biologists to move away from ideas that have either become obsolete or were incorrectly interpreted in the past. They are particularly up in arms against many popular scientific (mis)interpretations. Consider, for example, the complaint made by the victims of hurricane Katrina in New Orleans, who asked why they had been "left behind like animals", a complaint quoted in national and international media the following day. It says a lot about the way we view nature, but in fact animals do not necessarily leave each other behind during a crisis. The 'ape in us' is much more humane than we sometimes think.[12] Every discussion of human society makes huge assumptions about human nature. Such assumptions are often presented as if they come right out of a biology class where, in fact, they rarely belong.

Yes, we are social animals who are driven by incentives and focused on status, territory, victory and survival. But precisely because we are social animals, our human nature is also cooperative, empathic and equipped with a sense of justice. In fact, our biological ancestors, who determine this 'human' nature, spent about 95% of their time in collaborative activities. They did not survive by keeping everything for themselves or eliminating others. They survived by cooperating and sharing.

Back to apes... in an experiment where melons were given to only a limited number from a larger group, the lucky apes shared the melons around, so that everyone got something to eat. In fact this prompted the cameraman who filmed the experiment to exclaim: 'I wish my children could see this! They might actually learn something!' 'Fairness' also plays a role in social behaviour in apes. If you give two apes a different reward for performing the same task, the ape that is offered the smallest reward will invariably refuse it – just like most humans would.

It is for this reason that De Waal claims that aggression is not our only innate characteristic. We are also born with a number of mechanisms that allow us to cooperate with others, keep conflicts under control, channel hostility and solve problems. These mechanisms are just as natural as our aggressive tendencies. Of course, competition and the right of the strongest are also a part of the same story, but people cannot survive in exclusively competitive conditions. If conflict is the only valid strategy for survival, at the end of the day only the very strongest will survive, enjoying a very lonely existence! Fortunately, we have a choice: a choice between the belligerent or the cooperative sides of our nature. Which side will we choose? Which side do we want to nourish and strengthen?

Economists and political scientists frequently base their collaboration and interaction models on a supposed never-ending struggle in nature. Moreover, on the basis of these simplistic assumptions they then make prescriptive deductions about the type of negotiating behaviour that is realistic and successful. As a result, we often fall victim to a self-fulfilling prophecy. If you are convinced that man is defined by the 'survival of the fittest' paradigm, you will negotiate from this perspective. After all, you would not want to appear naïve. In this way you further confirm the paradigm.

What we need is another paradigm – a new and more intelligent way of negotiating.

This in turn requires a radical review of our assumptions about human nature and the basic attitudes and convictions from which we negotiate. After all, negotiation is not just a way to reach joint decisions on matters of common interest. It is also a habit. A habit is defined by three different dimensions: what we think (our convictions), what we know (our knowledge) and what we can do (our skills).

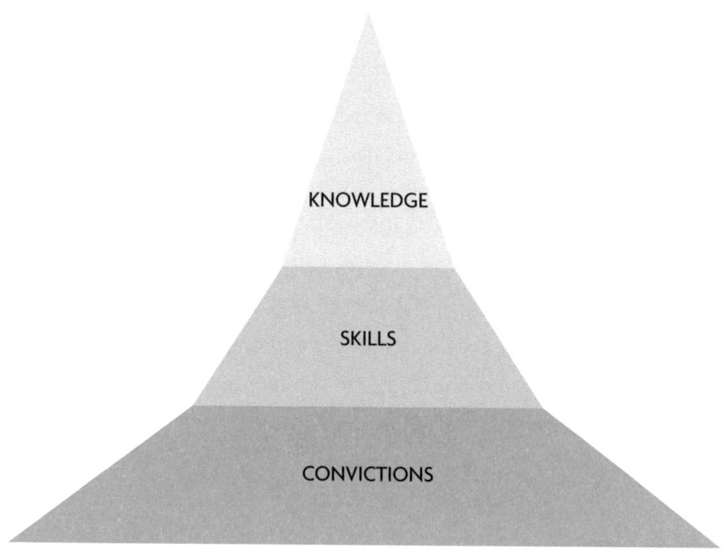

Our convictions form the basis for our habits. They determine how we use our knowledge and skills. In turn, our skills are the outward expression of our knowledge in practice. It is therefore not sufficient to know what we should do differently. We also need to know *how* we can do it differently. And we must also be convinced that this different way of doing things is better.

To negotiate more intelligently, we need to change our negotiating habits. This implies that we need to adjust all three dimensions.

NEGOTIATING IN STYLE – THE NEW NEGOTIATING CULTURE

The habitual negotiating behaviour of a person is characterized by a personal style or strategy. What are the most common styles and what do they mean for your negotiating strengths and development opportunities? Which strategy leads to smarter negotiation?

We can position the different negotiating styles on two universal negotiating dimensions: the level of importance you attach to your negotiating objective against the level of importance you attach to your negotiating relationship (see the schedule below).[13]

It is along these two axes that negotiators follow their own negotiation pathways. Imagine that your partner want to spend your holidays at the seaside, whereas you want to go to the mountains. You are goal-oriented. You always go 100% for your objectives and you are not afraid to impose your opinion on others. Consequently, you will act assertively to ensure that that your holiday takes place in the Alps rather than in Biarritz – besides, you know that your partner will really love it when you get there!

If, however, your relationship is your primary concern and if you are someone who likes to ensure harmony, you will be more likely to give in. ('If it makes you happy, it makes me happy; so let's go to the seaside.')

If you suggest a week by the sea and a week in the mountains, you are a compromise-seeker. If you find all these discussions about holiday destinations tiresome or you want to avoid conflicts at all costs, you may just try to avoid taking a decision – hopefully things will sort themselves out.

In these examples we can quite easily recognise a few different types of negotiator: the attacker, the pleaser, the compromiser and the avoider. While some of our behaviour depends on the specific situation, each of us is inclined to use one particular style more readily, more comfortably and more frequently than others. This preference – which is often unconscious – has its origins in our personality, our upbringing and our experience.

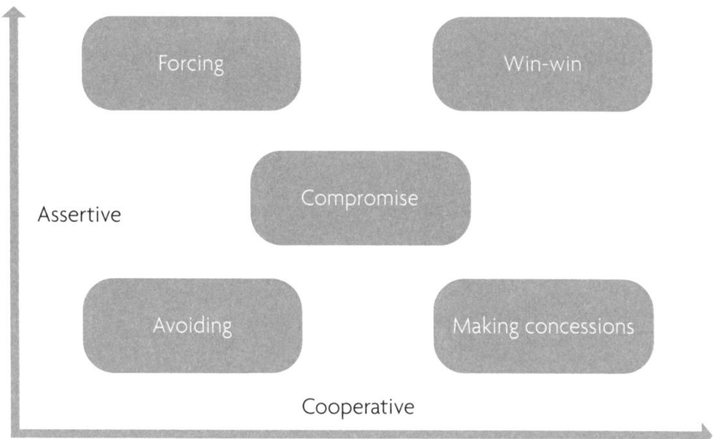

Each negotiating style has advantages and disadvantages. An attacker may regularly win if his style has no future implications – for example, if he is negotiating to buy a house (the chances that he will buy a house more than once from the same person are very small). He will also be effective in crisis management or when dealing with absolute priorities – the 'must-haves' of negotiations.

Of course, there is a price tag to aggressive negotiations in terms of relationships. If the level of mutual dependence among the negotiating parties is high, an aggressive approach will have a negative effect on negotiating results in the long term. The other party may eventually feel that he is being put under pressure to concede more than is reasonable, so that he decides to break off the negotiations entirely. In these circumstances, the attacker will be left behind with empty hands. Perhaps it is wiser to take heed of the following advice: "My father said: 'You must never try to make all the money that's in a deal. Let the other fellow make some money too, because if you have a reputation for always making all the money, you won't have many deals'." (John Paul Getty).

THE ATTACKER

"NEGOTIATIONS ARE A EUPHEMISM FOR CAPITULATION, IF THE SHADOW OF POWER IS NOT CAST ACROSS THE BARGAINING TABLE."

(George Schultz)

The attacker's objectives are sacred. He wants to win at all costs, even if this risks jeopardizing his relationship with the other side. He is competitive and likes to push through his own desires, if necessary to the point of aggressiveness. He is prepared to intimidate, threaten and use trick questions to try and throw his negotiating partner off balance. Similarly, he seeks fallacies in the other side's arguments. For him, negotiation is a question of winning or losing. There is no middle ground.

The pleaser is prepared to lose, if this allows him to maintain harmonious relations with the other side. This can sometimes be a good investment, which creates a valuable reserve of goodwill. This is particularly true in negotiations where the subject under discussion is more important for his negotiating partner than for himself or in situations where he knows he is wrong or has no real perspective of making progress. However, it is important not to overdo things. It is nice to have goodwill, but the pleaser risks living his life in poverty if he adopts this style too often.

THE PLEASER

'THE ONE SURE WAY TO CONCILIATE A TIGER IS TO ALLOW ONESELF TO BE DEVOURED.'

(Konrad Adenauer)

The pleaser is the opposite of the attacker. For him, the relationship is the most crucial thing, and this is where he invests his time and effort, even if this works to the disadvantage of himself and his own objectives. Harmony and the preservation of the relationship are more important than a fair negotiation outcome. The pleaser therefore adopts a lose-win style.

The avoider simply runs away from difficult situations. Sometimes, this can be a useful strategic approach. Consider, for example, the Cuban Missile Crisis in 1962, when the Americans discovered that the Soviet Union was attempting to install nuclear weapons in communist Cuba. The archives show that at one point during the crisis the Russian president, Nikita Khrushchev, sent two telex messages to his American counterpart, John F. Kennedy. One offered a possible way to avoid an escalation of the conflict while the other offered no hope of a peaceful settlement. Kennedy simply ignored the second telex and only answered the first one. It worked, with both sides making important concessions as a result. In other words: it is sometimes possible to steer a debate in a positive direction by ignoring some of the things your negotiating partner says and focusing instead on other, more positive comments. However, if you consistently avoid the key matters, you may miss crucial opportunities or, even worse, allow problems to grow uncontrollably and as such make them only more difficult to solve in the future.

THE AVOIDER

'DIPLOMACY IS MORE THAN SAYING OR DOING THE RIGHT THINGS AT THE RIGHT TIME; IT IS AVOIDING SAYING OR DOING THE WRONG THINGS AT ANY TIME.'

(Bo Bennett)

The avoider invests in neither the relationship nor the negotiating outcome. He understands the art of waiting, of diplomatically steering away from delicate subjects and of postponing challenges. He has the ability to pull out of a threatening situation. But he rarely makes it to the negotiating table. His motto is: 'he who fights and runs away, lives to fight another day.'

The compromiser steers towards quick decisions by formulating solutions that are acceptable to large numbers of parties to a debate. This is often what happens, for example, in the United Nations. The major disadvantage of this is that no one ends up fully satisfied with the resulting compromise. Compromises are rarely sustainable. The results are sub-optimal with much of the potential for achievements left unutilised. A classic example concerns the endless discussions on federal state reforms in Belgium: compromises are occasionally reached, but the heart of the matter is never satisfactorily solved.

THE COMPROMISER

'EVER NEGOTIATE WITH LAWYERS AT A HUGE COMPANY? IF THEY SAW YOU DROWNING 100 FEET FROM THE SHORE, THEY'D THROW YOU A 51-FOOT ROPE AND SAY THEY WENT MORE THAN HALFWAY.'

(Paul Somerson)

For the compromiser, the relationship and the outcome are both important, but to a limited degree. The compromiser seeks to find solutions that will keep everyone happy by splitting the differences between them. This means making concessions or adopting a middle position. It can lead to quick results, but only satisfies the interests of the negotiating parties in part, never in full.

Unfortunately, we tend to think that we can only optimize one dimension at the expense of another dimension. If we focus on our objectives, we will damage our relationships. If we focus on our relationships, we will damage our objectives.

But does this thought actually correspond with the reality? Is there no negotiating method or style that will allow us to take account of both relationships and our objectives? A style that will keep us at the negotiating table until we reach a solution that offers maximum possible benefit to both sides? The four negotiating styles mentioned above keep us trapped in a cycle of distributive negotiations: we are only concerned with how we can share the available cake and not with the key question: how can we increase the size of the cake? Negotiation is about more than merely solving problems. Negotiation is first and foremost about creating value and opportunities. But how can we do this?

WIN-WIN AND NEGOTIATION INTELLIGENCE (NQ®)

'ANY BUSINESS ARRANGEMENT THAT IS NOT PROFITABLE TO THE OTHER PERSON WILL IN THE END PROVE UNPROFITABLE FOR YOU. THE BARGAIN THAT YIELDS MUTUAL SATISFACTION IS THE ONLY ONE THAT IS APT TO BE REPEATED.'

(B.C. FORBES)

The answer to the above question is to be found in the concept of mutual gain or win-win negotiations. While every style has its merits, if used consciously and with reference to the specific circumstances, only the win-win style can produce optimal results for all parties at the negotiating table. This is certainly the case if the negotiations in question are not just a one-off event, but are part of a process that is repeated in the future.[14]

While win-win is familiar territory, it is also territory where hardly anyone knows the way. Many people forget that win-win means that you must actually help the other side to win too. The main difficulty with win-win is that you need to be strong in both dimensions: you must be both objective-oriented and relation-oriented. And you need to reach further along both axes than a compromiser. In other words, you must be able to generate added value both for yourself and for your negotiating partner. The only way to do this, is to increase your negotiation intelligence: your NQ(®).

What does negotiation intelligence involve? Many of us are familiar with emotional intelligence (EQ). Daniel Goleman concluded that the Harvard alumni with the highest IQ were not generally the happiest. He went in search of the missing link and found it in the shape of EQ, which plays a much more important role in determining people's happiness. In this context, he defined EQ as the capacity to deal effectively with our own feelings and the feelings of others.[15]

NQ® implies a capacity to transform our existing negotiating habits (our convictions, knowledge and skills) into a win-win approach. NQ® is the ability to see negotiations as an opportunity to proactively create new value, both in terms of objectives and relationships, while at the same time determining the rules and nature of the game.

THE NQ®-ER

'ONE'S MIND, ONCE STRETCHED BY A NEW IDEA, NEVER REGAINS ITS ORIGINAL DIMENSIONS.'

(Oliver Wendell Holmes)

An intelligent negotiator will improve the negotiating relationship and achieve, perhaps even exceed, his objectives. Of all the different types of negotiator, he is the one who best knows how to create the most added value.

NEGOTIATION: PROWESS OR PROFICIENCY?

Can we develop our NQ®? After all, not everyone is a gifted negotiator. Is the other side of our biological story – the ability to negotiate and cooperate – something that is only given to the happy few, like the female ape in our example above, or is it something that we can learn? Looking at biology for advice, we can find some interesting clues. When two different species of monkey are put together – one of them peaceable, such as the stump-tailed macaque, and the other more aggressive, such as the rhesus monkey – they quickly learn from each other. When allowed to live side by side over a long period, the rhesus monkeys will gradually become more conciliatory. Interestingly, once they are separated from the stump-tailed macaques again, they remain more conciliatory. In other words, this shows that the mechanisms which defuse conflict and encourage negotiation can be learnt. In the example of the monkeys they even are nature's preferred mechanisms.

Since the 1960s, theorists have been busy analyzing the characteristics of a good negotiator. It soon became apparent that these qualities could indeed be learnt. At the present time, negotiation courses are very popular in business schools, universities and companies. Why? Because in our increasingly complex, diverse and dynamic world, negotiation is seen as the most practical and efficient way to deal with scarce resources and differences and to avoid potential conflict.

One of the most common prejudices we encounter is the belief that people are either good or bad negotiators by nature and that consequently there is not very much you can do about it. Research has now shown that this is simply not true.[16] We *can* change our NQ®. We can learn it, just like any other skill. Compare it to swimming: those with a natural talent that train hard can become champions. But even those with little natural talent can get a long way by working hard and developing the right technique.

If we wish to gain access to the richness that NQ® can offer, we first need to find the right keys. This book describes four of these keys, each based on years of practical experience. Best practice and academic insights will be our travel guide on the road to NQ®. These four keys can make the difference between conflict escalation and straightforward bargaining on the one hand, and intelligent negotiation on the other hand. They are the basis of NQ®.

In Part I the keys will be translated, one by one, into a series of practical tools.

With the four keys, we offer a systematic and effective approach that will allow you to become the best negotiator you can possibly be.

1

KEYS TO INTELLIGENT NEGOTIATION

KEY 1: FREE YOURSELF FROM ENTRENCHED POSITIONS

'THE ONLY TRUE VOYAGE OF DISCOVERY... WOULD NOT BE TO VISIT NEW LANDSCAPES, BUT TO POSSESS OTHER EYES, TO SEE THE UNIVERSE THROUGH THE EYES OF ANOTHER...'

(Marcel Proust)

HOW ENTRENCHED POSITIONS CAN TAKE CONTROL OF YOU

'AS LONG AS YOU KEEP A PERSON DOWN, SOME PART OF YOU HAS TO BE DOWN THERE TO HOLD HIM DOWN, SO IT MEANS YOU CANNOT SOAR AS YOU OTHERWISE MIGHT.'

(Marian Anderson)

Mark Conway, the managing director of a respected production company, wants to sell his company. After discussing the matter with friends and experts, he sets a selling price of 60 million euros. There are plenty of interested candidates, but none of them want to fork out 60 million. The best offer Conway receives is 40 million. He is not willing to accept. He has the best directors and producers, he has successful series that will continue to run for years, and there is an important deal with Germany in the pipeline. But the candidate-buyers see things differently. Viewed from their perspective, the staff are too settled, the content lacks innovation and the price is not competitive. In short, they see a company that has passed its 'sell-by' date. A company that is worth no more than 40 million.

Conway might be winding down to retirement, but he is not prepared to take this lying down. He opts for a forceful negotiating approach. Encouraged by his boldness, the other parties respond in kind. The louder Conway shouts, the louder his potential buyers shout back. The negotiations turn into a duel – almost a matter of honour, with the opposing parties entrenched at 60 million and 40 million respectively.

What happened here? Why did these negotiations get stuck? Why was no one able to bring convincing arguments into play? The negotiators allowed themselves to get carried away by the myth of the right of the strongest. They see the negotiating process as the absolute power struggle of a predator and its prey. The strongest will win. The fittest will survive. The only choice for the other party is the classic 'fight or flight'. The object of the negotiation is not simply to divide up the cake, but to grab it all. If you can do this, you are a shrewd negotiator. Your opponent is the loser – the prey.

In this kind of 'zero-sum' or distributive negotiation, your aim is to keep as much as you can for yourself and give as little as possible to your negotiating partner. In reality, it is often the result of ignorance or short-sightedness: the negotiators dig themselves into entrenched positions because they are unable to see beyond the limits of their own negotiating arguments.

This is exactly what has happened with Conway and his take-over candidates. Both parties rapidly took up fixed positions, almost without thinking. Conway wants 60 million euros; the potential buyers only want to pay 40 million. And once they have taken their positions, the only thing they can do is to keep on defending them. As a result, they are unable to broaden their vision, which would allow them to look beyond the immediate problem in the hope of finding a possible solution. Instead, they both seek arguments and excuses to justify their widely differing prices. Whereas in the beginning they had at least some understanding for each other's position (after all, they both want the production company to survive) they are now miles apart. In these circumstances, even the smallest concession is seen as a sign of weakness, involving considerable loss of face. They simply keep on repeating the same arguments, thereby digging themselves deeper and deeper into their own positions. The situation degenerates into trench warfare, with everyone bogged down and no one capable of moving.

DISMANTLING ENTRENCHED POSITIONS

'PEACE CANNOT BE KEPT BY FORCE. IT CAN ONLY BE WON, THROUGH UNDERSTANDING. OUR LONGING FOR UNDERSTANDING IS ETERNAL.'

(Albert Einstein)

Harry Smith is one of Conway's biggest competitors. Smith has built up a major business empire and is also the owner of a number of successful production companies. He is one of the potential buyers at the negotiating table, and he would dearly love to take over his rival's company. A mood of near indifference descends on Conway.

Smith opens the discussion. He asks Conway what he really wants. How does he see the future of the production companies and what does he think is important? Where does he see new opportunities and what makes the company so valuable in his opinion? Does he want to remain personally involved in the future of the company? Conway explains calmly that he just wants a fair price for the production company that he has spent thirty years building up, a company that he cherishes like his own child. He is worried that staff cuts will follow. There are some potentially interesting contacts with Japan, which deserve to be followed up. He no longer wants final responsibility for the company, but he would still like to be involved in the major strategic decisions. He is not up to date with the latest technologies, but he still has a wealth of practical experience that he would like to pass on.

Now what happens? A good conversation develops. It is even possible to speak of a degree of *rapprochement* between the two old rivals. How did Smith make this possible? He moved beyond 'positions' and started looking at 'interests'.[17] In other words, he has progressed from asking *what* both sides want to asking *why* they want it.

The only thing you can achieve on the basis of fixed positions is a splitting of the difference. It is essentially a tug-of-war. Bringing interests into the debate, you have the necessary ingredients to create added value. Also, when you discuss positions, you tend to look only at the symptoms of the problem, not its causes. You are like a doctor who prescribes aspirin, without asking why the patient has a headache in the first place.

Smith's approach is different. He sets out identifying challenges and potential stumbling blocks. He wants to map the various interests of the different parties and find the discussion angles, the issues, the problems and the opportunities. In short, he clearly states his own interests, but is also prepared to look at things from Conway's perspective.

FOCUSING ON INTERESTS

'KEEP IN MIND THAT THE BETTER YOU UNDERSTAND WHAT YOU WANT AND WHY YOU WANT IT, THE BETTER YOUR CHANCES WILL BE OF ACQUIRING IT.'

(Fred Jandt)

Imagine that you have two young children – two daughters who both want the last orange in the fruit basket.[18] This quickly develops into an all-or-nothing confrontation, in which one girl is likely to get everything and the other nothing. At this point, you arrive on the scene and ask what all the fuss is about. The shops are closed, the neighbours are out and you don't have an orange tree in the garden... So what do you do? As a fair and honest parent, you obviously cut the orange down the middle. This is a compromise solution: each of your daughters gets 50% of what they wanted. Neither of them is really satisfied, which of course is the curse of compromise thinking.

If you continue to act on the basis of positional thinking, you will be condemned to follow this unsatisfactory distributive approach, unless you can shift the focus away from the positions and towards the interests behind those positions. Instead of saying: "I want that orange" or, "I am only willing to give 40 million euros for your production company", try probing into the underlying motives by asking: "Why do you want that orange?" or, "Why do you only want to pay that amount?"

Perhaps one sister wants the juice to drink and the other wants the peel to bake a cake. Inquiring about their interests and spelling them out can suddenly open new possibilities. It is perfectly feasible to give one the juice and the other the peel. In this way, they both get 100% of what they want, without having to make concessions.

> Harry Smith has Key 1, the key to dismantling entrenched positions, firmly in his pocket. He will not be pinned down by a fixed price, but immediately shifts the focus to the needs and wishes of the other negotiating parties. He tries to understand the reasons behind their positions. Conway's main concern is the future of his production house and the job security of his employees. Smith makes this discussable but also makes clear where his own interests lie: he wants a merger to create growth and added value through diversity. By identifying their interests and giving them a name, Smith and Conway are able to escape from their polarising positions. This puts them on the road towards mutual understanding and a mutually beneficial solution. Smith suggests ways to guarantee the jobs of Conway's staff in a creative manner, Conway agrees to act as an external adviser and the possibility of paying the final agreed price in

instalments is explored. The likelihood that Smith and Conway will reach an agreement gets bigger and bigger all the time.

In a good diagnosis of the interests, non-monetary considerations quickly come to the surface. Precisely in these non-monetary considerations a lot of value can be found. But as soon as people start talking about money, they tend to lose sight of such considerations. Experience suggests that it is wiser to first discuss non-tangible, immaterial benefits, and only move on to the financial aspects once these have been agreed. As soon as Smith and Conway start to talk about actual figures, there is a real chance that they will no longer be able to talk about anything else.

Often the parties will discover that they have common interests. These may become the basis for an agreement, provide positive motivation and encourage trust, creating a belief that together they will be able to reach a mutually acceptable solution. For instance, in our case study it is evident that both sides wish to ensure a bright future for the production company. Negotiators usually have an eye for this kind of common interest but often overlook complementary interests, such as the juice and peel in our orange example. Yet, they are even more important. From differing, yet complementary interests, the most value can be distilled but we tend to insufficiently exploit these differences.

When positions and even interests at first appear to be irreconcilable (as in the case study, where the highest bid is considerably lower than the asking price) a detailed interests analysis can sometimes open new perspectives. Consider the thorny subject of wage negotiations. Instead of focusing exclusively on the level of pay, it can be useful to highlight other factors, such as a more comfortable lifestyle, increased purchasing power, greater status, etc. This might lead to a proposal for more leave days instead of more pay, or a better job title, or greater flexibility in the choice of work locations.

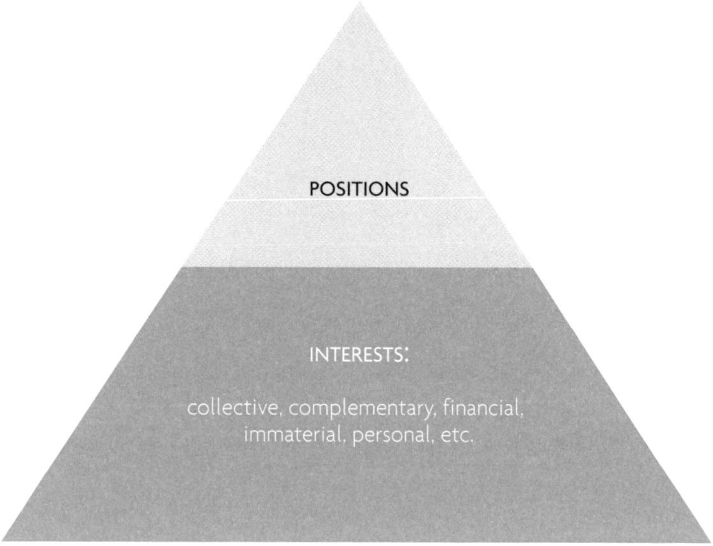

POSITIONS

INTERESTS:

collective, complementary, financial, immaterial, personal, etc.

HOW DO YOU FIND OUT ABOUT INTERESTS?

'MUCH OF WHAT NEGOTIATORS MUST DO TO CREATE AND CAPTURE VALUE DEPENDS ON THEIR ABILITY TO OBTAIN INFORMATION FROM THE OTHER SIDE.'

(Deepak Malhotra & Max Bazerman)

To make the transition from positions to interests, you must therefore step away from the power struggle and put an end to the tug-of-war that characterizes most negotiations. But there is more to it than you might think. You need to be aware that your efforts to search for a correct diagnosis of the conflict and to look at things from the perspective of your negotiating partner can be undermined by your naïve realism, which automatically colours your thinking. Naïve realism is the perception that:

1 we see things objectively, the way they really are, and that our actions are based on a rational interpretation of reality;

2 if others fail to share our interpretation, they are irrational and of bad faith.[19] (Ross & Ward, 1996).

In other words, we allow little room for the subjectivity of conflicts. We believe that we know what the other person thinks, feels, wants and needs, but in reality, each of the parties will take a different version of reality as their starting point, will select other facts as relevant, and will interpret those facts differently. Naïve realism thus contaminates our negotiations with false assumptions. And assumptions are the fly in the ointment of every negotiating strategy and the biggest enemy of every negotiator. Assumptions set people off on the wrong foot and in the past have even led to wars. They always come at a heavy price.

We are all trained in 'either...or' thinking. Either you are right or I am right ('my way or the highway'). The intelligence of good negotiators is based on their ability to consider two seemingly contradictory visions at the same time.[20] In order to use Key 1 in an effective manner, we need to train ourselves in 'and...and' thinking: "Taking your interpretation, your interests and my interests as a starting point, how can we understand what is happening here and what possibilities does it open up?"

We need to switch from a ('me-against-you') positional mindset to an interest-based 'we'-framework, so that we can invest our energy in understanding each other rather than 'in' competing with each other. After all, a position is nothing more than a solution that the negotiators have chosen – often hastily, sub-optimally and unconsciously – as a way to secure their interests. Interests are the implicit motivation behind this choice. Identifying and understanding these interests allows you to review whether the position you had taken originally was premature. It also allows you to see that you have many alternative and probably more productive choices at your disposal.

Excellent and intelligent negotiators with a high NQ® are driven by genuine curiosity. They accept that they do not possess the truth and that it is impossible to know the interests of the other party in advance. They are also convinced that a better understanding of these interests can often lead to surprising new insights. Their basic attitude is an exploratory attitude, and attitude of appreciative inquiry. They try to establish the real interests of their negotiating partner, without judgment or manipulation.[21]

Interests, however, do not manifest themselves of their own accord. People tend to be reluctant about giving information. Nevertheless, research has shown that you can increase your results by 10% if you first let the other person know what your interests are. The following serves as an example.

In an experiment, a group of two parties was given the task of talking freely about their interests. In a second group, only one of the two parties was allowed to talk about their interests; the other party was told to keep quiet. In a third group, both parties were instructed to say nothing about interests. Who achieved the best results? The group where both parties were open about their interests achieved the most optimal results and scored much better than the group where everybody held their tongues. This was perhaps to be expected. More surprising, however, was the fact that group where only one of the parties talked about their interests also scored significantly better than the 'silent' group. In other words, unilateral sharing of interests still allows you to perform better than the so-called 'clever' negotiators who keep information about their interests to themselves. This makes sense because if you stubbornly stick to your original position, you can expect nothing more than a share of the original cake.

So, intelligent negotiation with Key 1 involves an exploration of interests. Why does the other person want something? What need does this satisfy? What is he concerned about and what does he hope to achieve? Why does he feel this way? Why exactly is he demanding this, and not something else?

Many experienced negotiators believe that it is vital to discover what the other side wants. This sounds perfectly reasonable: how can you formulate a meaningful proposal if you don't know what your negotiating partner is hoping to achieve? For the same reason, you also spend quite a lot of time explaining to the other person exactly what you want.

Unfortunately, this can sometimes knock the negotiations off course. Too much focus on *what* people want means that we often fail to discover *why* they actually want it.

Imagine that you are waiting for a taxi outside in the cold. Just when you think your toes are about to freeze, you finally see a taxi approaching in the distance. The taxi driver stops for a red light and you hurry to meet him. To your dismay, he tells you that he has just finished his shift. You ask if he could do just one last trip, but you hardly get an answer. When you ask him why he is so unwilling, he tells you that he is urgently needed at home. Suddenly, you feel a dash of hope again! You ask if he will take you along if you both are heading in the same direction. You discover that your final destinations are fairly close to each other. Delighted, you jump into the back of the taxi. You arrive home without freezing even more and the driver earns a bit of extra money.

Something similar happened during the take-over discussions between Mark Conway and Harry Smith. Smith made a breakthrough when he asked why Conway wanted to sell his company and why he had particular demands to make about its future.

Here is another example. Following the 1967 war in the Middle East, the Israelis and the Egyptians were unable to agree on the terms of a peace treaty. Both sides wanted the same thing: possession of the

Sinai desert. There was deadlock until it became clear that Egypt wanted the Sinai so that it would not be seen to surrender territory and Israel wanted the Sinai to eliminate the risk of a surprise attack from that direction in the future. Once this was known, the solution was obvious. The Sinai became a demilitarized zone – and it still is today.

To use Key 1 intelligently, you need to have empathy. You need to put yourself in the other person's shoes, to see things from his point of view, to build up trust and rapport. You must be good at listening actively and asking empathically in order to maximise the chances of truly understanding the other side. You must also use your analytical skills to make the right diagnosis and to ensure that the building blocks for an agreement are available on the negotiating table.

SPEECH IS GOLDEN?

'ARE YOU REALLY LISTENING... OR ARE YOU JUST WAITING FOR YOUR TURN TO TALK?'

(R. Montgomery)

The experiment about expressing your interests shows that giving information to the other party works to your advantage. It provides the necessary ingredients for increasing the size of your cake and outlines the contours of the so-called ZOPA – the Zone of Possible Agreement.

It is logical that you can only trace the contours of this zone once both parties have made their wishes and intentions clear. Contrary to what most people think, success in negotiation is not dependent first and foremost on your powers of persuasion, but on your ability to listen. Information equals influence and impact!

Identify your ZOPA ZOne of Possible Agreement

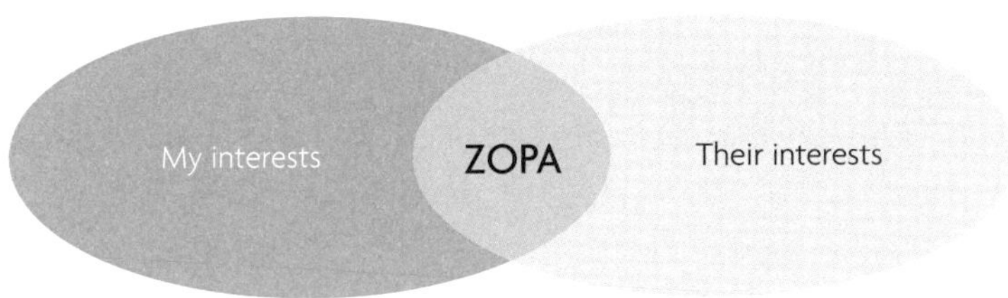

ZOPA contains overlapping interests

Even experienced negotiators operating in a field with which they are familiar need to find a new ZOPA each time they enter into major new negotiations. It is a misconception to believe that the ZOPA is a fixed area on a fictitious map, where NQ®-ers can navigate with their eyes shut. The best balance for you is to listen for 70% of the time and speak for just 30%. And by this we mean, of course, speaking about your interests.

While it is good to make your interests known from the outset, it is not advisable to talk about your limits too soon. For example, if you are unwilling to accept anything less than 1,200 euros in your next round of pay negotiations, it is not smart to explicitly mention this figure immediately. If you do, there is a good chance that you will get your 1,200 euros – but no more. Perhaps your boss was willing to give you 1,500. There is another risk: if you immediately get everything you ask for, without having to fight for it, you can still end up feeling dissatisfied, because you now realise that you could – and perhaps should – have asked for more. Your success came too easily but now it is too late to do anything about it.

The fear of getting what we want too quickly, sometimes referred to as the 'winner's curse', encourages a certain degree of caution when giving information (more about this in Key 3).

This leads to another question: is it really wise to be the first person to give information? Should you make the first move? Or should you let (or make) the other person go first? If we put this question to executives in our courses, the majority answer that you should never make the opening bid: you should keep your cards close to your chest and allow the other side to play their hand first. But is this really the right approach? As so often, the answer is dependent on the context. For example, if you don't know what kind of financial reward you can ask for a particular job, surely it is better to allow your prospective employer to make the opening offer? Imagine that you go first but make your pitch too high: you may be politely shown the door without being given a second chance to put things right. And the same is true if your pitch is too low: grossly undervaluing the job (and your own worth) can only create the wrong impression.

If the framework – the ZOPA – is unclear to you, it is better to let the other person go first. But if you are confident about your subject and the context, it is best to set your own anchor first. Because anchoring in this manner offers a crucial advantage. In most negotiations, the first bid remains the anchor point (or reference point) throughout the entire negotiating process. In this respect, the anchor point has a huge influence on the further development of the negotiations, since it sets the parameters for future discussion. As a result, the final outcome is frequently close to the original anchor point.

For this reason, an NQ®-er usually likes to make the first move, but he does not do this randomly or without careful thought. The anchor point has to be set realistically. If you make a proposal that goes far beyond the boundaries of any likely agreement, you may lose the trust and confidence of your negotiating partner, which is the very last thing you want. Worse, you may prompt him into making an equally arbitrary counter-proposal. To avoid escalation of this kind, you need the right background information. And how do you get this? Exactly! By asking the right questions and giving the right information. You do this gradually, moving forward one step at a time. In this way, you can reduce risk to a minimum. If your conversation partner is reluctant to talk about a certain point, you can easily pull back or change the subject. The intelligent negotiator also explains why he asks particular questions. In this way, he avoids being seen as an inquisitor by the other person.

With key 1 to a higher NQ®, you know that...

... you must focus on underlying INTERESTS and avoid fixating on POSITIONS. A position is a concrete demand or claim. It always has a polarising effect. Maintaining fixed positions means that you will be condemned to distributive compromise thinking. You must free yourself from the idea that negotiation is a power struggle, where the objective is to obtain the biggest piece of the cake. Instead, you must try to make everybody's interests visible and discussable. An interest is a need or a desire and expresses why something is important. Identifying interests and articulating them helps to release people from the restrictions and limitations of polarising positions. It brings you to the heart of the problem and sets you on the road towards mutual understanding and a mutually beneficial solution. As a smart negotiator you also know that LISTENING is more important for final success than your powers of persuasion. You have EMPATHY for the other person and GENUINE CONCERN for his interests.

The following tips can help you to dismantle entrenched positions and increase your NQ®:

- Define your OBJECTIVES and IDENTIFY challenges and potential stumbling blocks.
- Keep an OPEN MIND, so that you can avoid polarising positions.
- Make sure that everyone's interests are brought out and then explore them thoroughly. They are the most important ingredients for creating added value.
- Use an interest-based 'we'-framework. Do not think 'either...or'. Think 'and...and'.
- Discuss immaterial interests before you start talking about financial matters.
- Common interests are a strong motivating factor. Identify them.
- Don't lose sight of complementary interests. These often contain the greatest added value.
- Sketch the contours of the ZOPA but do not immediately reveal your own limits.

KEY 2: UNLOCK HIDDEN VALUE

'WOULD YOU RATHER CLAIM 50% OF A 200 EURO PIE OR 50% OF A 100 EURO PIE?'

(Malthotra & Bazerman)

Can you still remember the entrenched bickering from first 'discussions' about the take-over of the Conway production company? Both sides had fixed their ideas on a portion of the cake to which they felt they were entitled. Their valuation of the situation was the most rational interpretation of reality. This obstructive approach only changed when the discussions moved on to a consideration of interests and the negotiators drew up an inventory of what exactly everyone wanted and why. This suddenly allowed common interests to be identified.

The difference (in style) is obvious. You have *value-claimers* and *value-creators.*[22] Value-claimers operate in the bottom left-hand corner of the following diagram. Here, we often find ourselves when negotiating. This is the negotiating practice of the bazaar – the zero-sum negotiation. The combined total of our negotiation results is always zero. If I give you ten of something, I lose ten of something. And vice versa. The size of the cake is fixed. All that needs to be decided is who gets the biggest piece. And so we begin to haggle and barter, as if we were in the souk in Cairo or Istanbul. We see it as our task to reduce the distance between the respective positions, rather than to increase the number of possibilities and thereby the overall size of our cake.

The value creators work in the top right-hand corner of the diagram.

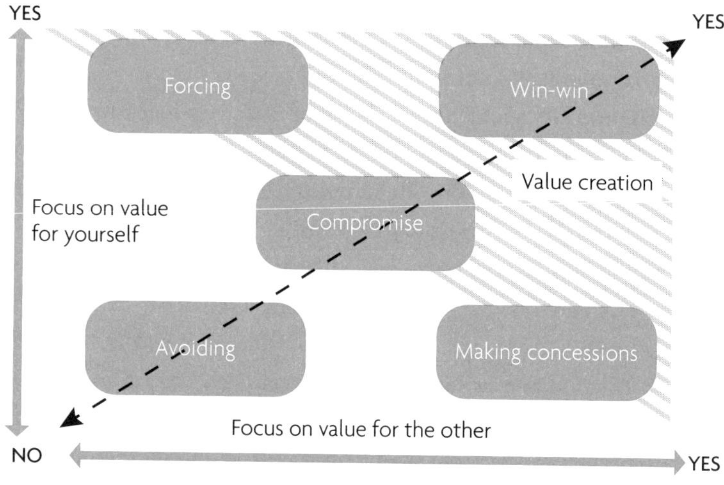

How can we arrive at win-win solutions that optimise both results and relationships? We have already identified our mutual interests. Is it possible to use these interests to first increase the size of our cake – to create added value – and then share it out equitably? If so, why don't we just do it?

PATTERN-BREAKING THINKING

'OUR MIND IS NOT IN THE BOX. THE BOX IS IN OUR MIND. WE CREATE THE BOX OURSELVES.'

(Nick Souter)

To be fair on us, it is not entirely our fault that we find this difficult. In the course of human evolution, we have developed a powerful and efficient way of thinking that allows us to process a multiplicity of complex information. In particular, we have developed patterns of thinking that enable us to recognize clusters of data. If these patterns are successful – in other words, if they help us to make the right choices or perform the right actions – we store them away in our memories, so that they can be used again in comparable situations. This happens through a mechanism that allows our brain cells to pass on signals to other brain cells. They do this through a series of nerve connections that become stronger the more often they are used. In time, these connections become so strong and their patterns so firmly embedded that we use them as *short cuts* for dealing with certain recognizable problems.

Eventually, we react automatically in these situations. This is an advantage, since it allows us to focus our conscious attention on new circumstances and challenges. In this way, thinking patterns become thinking habits. Our 'experience' is therefore the total sum of all these different patterns. Anyone who has ever learnt to drive a car will understand how this process works. At first you have to do everything consciously – indicator on, slip throttle, clutch in, change gear, turn wheel, and so on. But after a while you do all these things almost without thinking – so much so that you can listen to the news on the radio or engage in deep conversation while cruising. The actual driving of the car has become an automatism.

Our thinking 'machine' is quick and efficient, precisely because of the stability of its patterns and habits. For this reason, we are not inclined to easily give up these habits. Imagine that you find yourself in a situation where you are required to drive differently – for example, in a country where cars drive on the opposite side of the road. It requires great concentration not to automatically return to your 'normal' side of the road, certainly if you are changing from one road to another. But we can do it, if we try. In other words, creative or pattern-breaking thinking must (and can!) be learnt. Must – because the ZOPA in negotiations is frequently zero or even negative, so it needs to be consciously created if we want the negotiations to proceed.

Imagine, for example, that the difference between what is offered and paid is so great that one of the parties has to make a huge concession to reach an agreement. This is not win-win. At best it is win-lose. Perhaps it is even lose-lose. At first glance, you would say that this is an absolute 'no-go'.

Consider the case of a pharmacist's delivery service that drives around town all day, delivering medicines. They would like to switch to electric vans, since this is in keeping with their vision of a 'healthy' urban environment – an image they are keen to promote. They can even draw state subsidies to assist the change-over. A manufacturer of such vans is offering interesting terms, since they are keen to break into the medical sector. Yet in spite of a positive social climate and the willingness of all parties to look constructively at the financial aspects, an agreement cannot be reached. The budget of the delivery service is still too small and the manufacturer cannot be expected to sell his vehicles at a loss. In other words, there is no zone of possible agreement.

Both parties are disappointed, because they are keen to work together. So everybody puts on their thinking caps to see if some way can be found to save the project. A brainstorming session produces new ideas, such as the paid participation of a knowledge centre that can test the batteries, sponsoring by third parties or a search for other project partners. Then the delivery service mentions that their vehicles are only on the road for about 20% of the time. The medicines are mostly delivered in the morning. For the rest of the day, there are only a few emergency deliveries to be made. Someone suggests that there are several other types of organization that require transport for only a limited part of the day: child care centres, rest homes, libraries with more than one branch, etc. Maybe they would be prepared to participate? Moreover, the delivery service has good contacts with colleagues in other towns and with the medical sector in general, and they too seem interested in taking part in the project. Now, there is a whole new plan on the table for organising to share the electric vans. More and more partners are found, producing a snowball effect. The vehicles carry slogans or publicity banners to increase the visibility of the participants. The original chemist's delivery service saves a huge amount on costs and sees its original version taken to a level that it had not even dreamt of when it launched the original idea. The vehicle manufacturer gets access to the medical sector, as well as greater name recognition and increased profits from the larger scale of the final project.

NEGOTIATION PROBLEMS AS GOLDEN EGGS

'ALL TRUTH PASSES THROUGH THREE STAGES: FIRST IT IS RIDICULED, SECOND IT IS VIOLENTLY OPPOSED, AND THIRD IT IS ACCEPTED AS SELF-EVIDENT.'

(Arthur Schopenhauer)

Our mental 'short cuts' are very useful for our daily functioning. They allow us to make decisions quickly. But they also have one major disadvantage: if we need to think creatively or in a pattern-breaking manner, if we want to wander away from the familiar paths, it requires considerable and conscious mental effort to bypass the short cut mechanism. We first need to question the mechanism's validity in the existing situation. Is the solution that we normally use in these circumstances the only possible one? Is it the right one? Are there no better alternatives? The fact that this process has a neuro-physiological basis means that pattern-breaking negotiation is a serious challenge. But there is also a silver lining: the same neuro-physiological basis means that creative thinking is also a mechanism that can strengthen itself through frequent use.[23]

Our capacity to make snap judgements actually hinders us in this very change. Ideas that are new or far from obvious often seem at first glance to be 'unattainable', 'unrealistic', 'impractical' or 'ill-conceived'. We have a tendency to close our minds to such ideas. They feel uncomfortable, different, strange, risky. And so we are quick to condemn them, without giving them much conscious thought. ("That won't work in our company." "We've already tried it." "You'll never convince senior management." "My negotiating partner will never accept that.") Such reactions are the kiss of death for creative thinking: new ideas are smothered in the cradle before they are ever given a chance to grow. Think about the brainstorming sessions you have taken part in and try to remember just how difficult it is not to respond automatically to every new idea with: "Yes, but..."

If we want to negotiate intelligently, we must think in terms of opportunities rather than difficulties. In our culture, the word 'problem' has negative connotations. Problems bring difficulties – and so we associate them with failure. In Japan, however, problems are seen as 'golden eggs'. They bring good luck if you find one.[24] This encourages a totally different attitude. A problem is seen as a chance to improve something, often through a process of negotiation, since negotiation is concerned with reconciling the differences between people that lead to problems. To put it another way: negotiating is about the creation of opportunities. Or at least it should be. Instead of focusing on the past and on the proposals already on the table, we should be concentrating on the future and searching for the proposals that have not yet been made.

NEGOTIATING IN THE FEAR-FREE ZONE

'A THOUGHTLESS REMARK OR JUST THE SHRUG OF A SHOULDER CAN CRUSH A BRILLIANT THOUGHT BEFORE IT HAS THE CHANCE TO DEVELOP AND BECOME A NEGOTIATION BREAKTHROUGH.'

(Nick Souter)

The first thing that an intelligent negotiator needs to do is to create a fear-free zone. Creativity and out-of-the-box thinking lead us into unknown territory and the unknown automatically provokes resistance, fear and disbelief.

A very successful Australian company has given its investment advisers a mandate to operate two parallel portfolios: a real one and an imaginary one. At the end of the year, the adviser is assessed in part on his performance in this second, fear-free zone.[25]

To negotiate creatively, you should preferably organize your negotiations in two phases: a first phase in which new ideas are generated and a second phase during which you evaluate these ideas thoroughly before committing to the best ones.

Separate the idea-creation process from the decision-making process! In negotiations it is important to create space in which you can generate imaginative solutions that bring together your own interests and the interests of your negotiating partner, but without the need for immediate commitment. The evaluation of the options and the final decision to commit to one or more of them occurs at a later stage. In the first instance, every idea must be seen as a potentially valid idea. Otherwise, you will never develop a new approach to your negotiating problems. Once you start judging, you stop imagining. Your thinking must be divergent (looking for alternatives) and not convergent (accepting the obvious). In this context, remember that just 20% of the information you use to create a new idea comes from outside sources; the remaining 80% is produced by your own brain!

In our earlier example with the orange, both sisters received 100% of their wishes only after they had revealed their underlying interests. Had they remained silent, they would have only received 50% each. But they can go even further and explore other interesting possibilities. Are there kiwis in the house, is there fruit juice in the fridge, or perhaps jam in the cupboard to bake a pie? By thinking divergently, you broaden the scope of the negotiations, multiplying the number of ingredients available so the overall size of your cake can be increased.

RULES FOR VALUE CREATION

There are a number of basic rules for generating added value in negotiating situations:

- Increase the size of the playing field. As long as you are negotiating about a single subject, your negotiations are inherently distributive. For example, if you only talk about salary (and not about other possible benefits), you will eventually arrive at a zero-sum situation. Adding new themes to the discussions is an important technique for creating additional value. More themes give you an increased number of different types of currency to trade on in accordance with different perceptions of value.
- Once you have increased the size of your playing field, you can organize *trade-offs* between the different value attributions or preferences. Each side can be given something that it badly wants in exchange for something that it regards as not so important. Imagine that Peter and Priscilla both collect stamps. Peter has long hoped to find a particular Swedish stamp, whereas he already has dozens from Norway. In contrast, Priscilla (who has the Swedish stamp that Peter wants) has been looking for a particular Norwegian stamp for ages, which Peter happens to have as a double in his collection. After serious negotiation, Priscilla agrees to swap the Swedish stamp for the Norwegian one, plus 100 euros. Both sides are happy. The swapped stamps had little value to their original owners, but considerable value to the new owners.
- You can increase value by changing the scale, scope and time horizon of the subjects under negotiation (which is what happened, for example, in our pharmacist delivery case).

The following table shows how value-creators differ from value-claimers.[26]

	VALUE-CLAIMERS	VALUE-CREATORS
RESULT	WIN-LOSE	WIN-WIN
MOTIVATION	INDIVIDUAL GAIN	MUTUAL GAIN
INTERESTS	INCOMPATIBLE	CONGRUENT
RELATION	SHORT TERM	LONG(ER) TERM
THEMES	SINGULAR	PLURAL
SOLUTIONS	NON-CREATIVE, DISTRIBUTIVE	CREATIVE, ENHANCING

The intelligence of good negotiators is based in part on their ability to create a third, superior idea from two seemingly incompatible initial ideas.[27] They do this in such a manner that none of the available value is left behind unused on the negotiating table. Funny – or tragically – enough, negotiators sometimes cling to unsatisfactory solutions from a kind of laziness or complacency (that can be compared with the short cuts discussed earlier). This is the problem of no problem. If people refuse to see a problem, if there is a clear ZOPA, they will opt for obvious solutions, which leave plenty of potential value lying wasted on the table. In other words, they are often prepared to blindly accept second-best options.

This is demonstrated by an interesting experiment.[28] If you allow spouses and dating couples to negotiate, you would expect them to achieve better results than people who do not know each other, since they have a stronger focus on a long-term relationship. Yet the opposite is true. The unknown pairs reach win-win solutions with much greater frequency, since the spouses and couples are more willing to accept mediocre proposals (which in the long run can actually lead to greater relational frustration). The strangers are better at concentrating on their ultimate aspirations and at considering new ways to satisfy these aspirations. In other words, the desire to make the other person happy – which is the main motivation of the spouses and couples – is not sufficient to reach a good solution. Indeed, NQ®, and in particular Key 2, is not a matter of altruism; it is the art and science of value creation. In order to claim value, you first need to create it.

Smith and Conway have sketched the first contours of a ZOPA of 5 million euros (between 45 and 50 million), a zone in which they might be able to come to an agreement. This is progress, since not so long ago the take over negotiations risked breaking down completely. But would it not be possible to increase the size of the ZOPA? Because the bigger the ZOPA, the greater the opportunity for trade-offs and value augmentation on both sides. As we have already seen, non-material matters can also play a role but they are often overlooked if the ZOPA is too limited and rigid. Key 2 helps to enlarge the ZOPA and Smith knows how to use this key. He puts a number of value-enhancing options on the table – options that are then supplemented by input from Conway. For example, Smith offers to pay more if he can pay on credit, rather than in cash. Or maybe the sale price can take account of the rate of interest and the payment schedule? Perhaps he can make a substantial advance payment? Above all, Smith reacts to the concerns that Conway has mentioned. As the previous owner, it might be possible for Conway to launch a number of new projects with a profit-sharing option. This would clearly be beneficial for Smith, whilst at the same time satisfying Conway's desire to maintain a link with 'his' company. In return, Conway might offer to introduce Smith to the most important contacts among his huge network in the sector. It would be a shame to allow this potential source of future influence to go to waste. One of Conway's main worries was the future of his staff. Perhaps Smith is prepared to give guarantees in return for financial concessions?

As a result of all these value-enhancing options, the ZOPA now has a very different, much more attractive look. There are many more ingredients on the table, both material and non-material, so that the ZOPA can be broadened by a further 10 million euros (to between 42 and 52 million).

With key 2 to a higher NQ®, you know that...

... there is a crucial difference (in style) between a value claimer and a value creator. The creation of options that offer added value for both parties is the hallmark of the NQ®-er. He is not shackled by the assumption that the cake has a fixed size. Instead, he tries to make the cake bigger, by searching for new opportunities and alternatives. He deals with challenges divergently. This intelligent, creative style of negotiation requires, amongst other things, the use of pattern-breaking thinking and broadening the field of vision so that it is no longer limited to just a single issue. Single issue negotiations are inherently distributive – and this is something the NQ®-er wishes to avoid. Instead, he is open to new suggestions, postpones judgment and thinks in terms of possibilities rather than difficulties. He will only move on to the commitment phase once all the different options have been thoroughly explored.

Moreover, the NQ®-er understands that it is fundamental to the success of Key 2 that you should not only attempt to secure your own gains, but must also help your negotiating partner to obtain his gains! Not out of altruism, but out of self-interest: by showing concern for the objectives of others, you will find it easier to achieve your own. And the more important a negotiation relationship is, the more important it becomes to negotiate win-win solutions. This offers the only way to escape haggling towards zero-sum negotiations with their perpetual dilemma: do you go for maximum gain or do you make concessions? The bigger the zopa, the greater the chance of trade-offs – and therefore of win-win.

As a value-creator, you understand the art of feeding the relationship *and* obtaining better results. This means that you will score consistently better in the longer term.[29]

The following tips can help you to unlock hidden value and increase your NQ®:

› Make the ZOPA and the negotiating field as big as possible.
› Be CREATIVE, leave the familiar pathways, think DIVERGENTLY and search for value-enhancing alternatives.
› Be OPEN to new ideas and suggestions, do NOT JUDGE too quickly, and work in the FEAR-FREE ZONE.
› Avoid laziness, complacency and short cuts. Try to achieve the best possible results.
› In short, become a VALUE-CREATOR, who seeks to ensure added value for all concerned.

KEY 3: OPEN YOUR SAFETY NET

Value claimers regard value creators as somewhat naïve. Their motto is to play hard and play to win and they often get their way. After all, not everyone possesses negotiating intelligence and there are still plenty of unsuspecting victims for the unscrupulous to prey on. You do not want to be that victim. So how can you use your NQ® to ensure that you don't become a casualty of your own constructive behaviour? The answer is to be found in Key 3. Key 3 is your safety net, which will not only prevent you from falling into a trap but will also allow you to collect (and optimize) your share of the gains.

As we saw earlier, the negotiations between Mark Conway and Harry Smith were initially characterized by a quite positive approach which allowed the two men to move closer to each other. Smith showed himself to be a good listener and gave the impression of being a win-win negotiator. As a result, Conway now finds himself in the following situation: because he has the feeling that his people and his production company are in good hands with Smith, he begins to hint that he might be willing to drop his asking price, perhaps even to a figure below the lower limit of the most recent ZOPA (42 million euros).

During this same phase, Smith begins to look increasingly worried, referring to the changing landscape in the broadcasting media. The budgets for productions continue to fall and there is greater competition than ever before for the 'viewing time' of consumers. Particularly the 'classic' companies like Conway's are vulnerable to the new trends, according to Smith. As a result of these arguments, Conway is inclined to lower his price still further – a safe future for his staff is more important than hitting the financial jackpot. In other words, what seemed like a win-win situation not so long ago, now seems to be turning into a win-lose situation, with Conway at the losing end.

THE ASPIRATION BASE

'THE BEGINNING POSITIONS ARTICULATED BY PEOPLE WHEN THEY NEGOTIATE SIGNIFICANTLY AFFECT THE FINAL TERMS THEY ACHIEVE.'

(Charles B. Craver)

Like Conway, many negotiators begin the negotiating process without a clear idea of their optimal result – their aspiration base. Yet, research has shown that the level of your initial aspirations often has a huge impact on the final outcome: negotiators who aim high score consistently better.[30] Even so, many of us apply self-censorship: "I don't dare to ask for this, that just won't wash, he will never agree..." In this way, we deny ourselves the opportunity to optimize our results and we leave little room for concessions. We do this because we are, by nature, risk-avoiders. We hate to run the risk of being refused or rejected. We are frightened of upsetting others. This is why it is so important to have a clear picture of the ZOPA: it allows you to aim high without making unacceptable proposals or jeopardizing the negotiating relationship. You can maximize your headroom while no 'shark' can compromise your results. Setting your anchor cleverly (see Key 1) is a good way to maximize your chances of achieving your aspirations.

THE BOTTOM LINE

'YOU MUST BE PREPARED TO LOSE A GREAT DEAL IN ORDER TO MAKE A GREAT DEAL.'

(Anonymous)

It is just as important to set a clear bottom line – the point at which you will leave the negotiating table. Without this crucial guideline, there is a risk that you will continue to negotiate to a point far below the minimum that makes sense for you. Many get blinded by the need to get 'something' out of the discussions in order to compensate for at least some of the time and effort invested. To guard yourself against this psychological mechanism, it is advisable to set a point of no return – your lowest possible limit – before you open the negotiations. It is equally important to stick to this limit, unless significant new information becomes available. If you fail to do this, a shrewd negotiating partner will be quick to sense the absence of a minimum position and will seek to exploit this ruthlessly. For this reason, it is typically necessary to show that you are approaching your lowest limit, and will break off the negotiations unless there is a change of course.

COVERING YOUR BACK: THE BATNA

'THE SINGLE MOST POWERFUL TOOL FOR WINNING A NEGOTIATION IS THE ABILITY TO GET UP AND WALK AWAY FROM THE TABLE WITHOUT A DEAL.'

(Anonymous)

It can be very difficult to respect your own lowest limit and to walk away from the negotiating table if you are unsure where this might lead. Nobody likes to leave towards a void. It is vital to ask yourself in advance how you will be able to solve the negotiating challenge if you are unable to reach agreement with your negotiating partner. In other words, what are the alternatives to a settlement? If you cannot answer this question, you inevitably risk negotiating until you are far below your lowest limit. Setting a 'Best Alternative To a Negotiated Agreement', a BATNA[31], can help you to define and respect this lowest limit. A BATNA is a reserve plan that will offer you an escape route if things don't turn out as planned. There always is such a plan B. We often use them intuitively.

For example, when buying a car we will usually check the prices at a number of different dealers. This allows us to set our BATNA and forms the basis for our negotiations for a better price with our preferred dealer. Our BATNA can be a decision to keep our old car, or have it repaired, or postpone the purchase until next year when a new model will have come out and the price will have fallen, or buy the new car from another dealer after all.

To a significant degree, your BATNA determines the strength of your position at the negotiating table. Imagine that Conway suddenly receives an unexpected telephone call from a surprise new candidate: this will strengthen his negotiating hand against Smith, since he now has a viable alternative. The stronger your alternative is, the more comfortable and confident you become. The more acceptable your no-deal option is for yourself, the more it acts as an encouragement to be ambitious in your negotiation objectives. Your BATNA is a kind of touchstone, the acid test against which you compare every agreement and your insurance that you will not be sold short. Because in theory your BATNA can never be lower than your lowest limit. Moreover, a BATNA also protects you against escalation of commitment. We mentioned this earlier: since you have already invested so much in the negotiations, you don't want to walk away without a deal, and so you continue to negotiate downwards and downwards. Surely anything is better than nothing? No, it isn't! Not always. Always bear in mind that no deal is sometimes the best deal.

Research has proven conclusively that to reveal your BATNA is just about the most stupid thing you can do.[32] If you make this mistake, the BATNA will act as a magnet for the other party and he will persist in making proposals that are only marginally better than your 'walk-away' position. Therefore, only mention your BATNA if it is a particularly strong one. If you do feel that you are in a position to raise the subject, do so in a manner that is not threatening. This would undermine your conversation partner's trust and will only help you if you foresee no future need for a relationship with this partner. And of course, don't forget to think about *his* BATNA.

Finally, you need to be aware that the absence of a BATNA means that you do not have a negotiating position. You will be at the mercy of the other party and all you can hope is that he is a win-win negotiator. In the worst case, a shrewd negotiator can push you well under your lowest limit with little you can do about it.

Your aspiration base, your lowest limit, the BATNA and the ZOPA determine the framework within which you can negotiate safely. In your preparations and during the actual negotiating process it is important to use Key 3 *after* Keys 1 and 2. In this way, the framework becomes all the richer, since it has been nourished by your interests and by added value creation.

DIVIDE AND RULE?

Even the best value-creator cannot be regarded as an intelligent negotiator if in the end he fails to return home without his share of the spoils. Sooner or later, the cake needs to be divided. Getting to this point after long negotiations in which you have avoided a conflict approach, are you now forced to play the power game after all? How can you avoid making arbitrary demands, which will seem unjustified in the eyes of your negotiating partner? Is it possible to use your NQ® to get around these problems? Fortunately, here too Key 3 can come to the rescue.

Look again the Conway-Smith negotiations. In their discussions about the take-over of the production company, they have managed to add other interests to the negotiating pot, but they remain fundamentally at odds over the sale price. Conway was first inclined to lower his price (too far), but after further thought he has now decided that this requires too big a sacrifice on his part. To get the negotiations back on a constructive course, it is now necessary for both parties to focus on the created value that is effectively on the table. This leads us to the crucial question: how is it possible to ensure that this value is divided fairly and satisfactorily?

EXTERNAL DISTRIBUTION CRITERIA

To settle the dispute over the sale price, the intelligent NQ®-er would familiarize Conway and Smith with scenarios and prices of other take-overs in their sector in both the domestic and international markets. He would examine the relevant (European) legislation and provide software models that can predict the likely financial consequences of any proposed deal. The second most important element of Key 3, next to setting and guarding your BATNA, is the clever distribution of the total value currently on the table. In this sense, Key 3 is not only your safety net. It is also the net that allows you to scoop up your fair share of the gains.

To make sure that this distribution is as beneficial as possible for all concerned, the NQ®-er will use Key 3 to apply and interpret external standards and points of reference that have so far been beyond the scope of the negotiations. These criteria are independent of the wishes of the negotiating partners and therefore make it feasible to achieve a rational distribution of value. This means that it is possible to avoid a power struggle in which the right of the strongest will prevail.

But what are these criteria, exactly? Can you appeal to just any external reference point? Are they all good? Not necessarily. External criteria are only good if they persuade the other person and protect your own position; if they produce a result that is to your advantage (or is at least not to your disadvantage); if they are reasonable, relevant and acceptable; and if you can explain them clearly and fully justify them. And this applies not only to you, but to all parties in the negotiations.

Equality is one of the criteria that is generally accepted. Something is reasonable if it applies to everyone and is applied across the board. In this sense, for example, you could ask an estate agent whether or not he used the contract he is proposing to you when he purchased his own house. Or in the words of Gary Friedman: 'You must be able to explain why something that is good for someone else is also good for you.'[33]

Another, less widely used, criterion is the level of contribution: whoever puts most in is entitled to get a little more out. But both contribution and need are notoriously difficult to measure so this reference point is not always practical. Other 'reasonable' criteria include precedent, market convention, academic or scientific opinion, developed standards and norms, best practice, etc.

It is not unusual for the criterion or a combination of different criteria to be the subject of considerable negotiation in their own right. What can be seen, however, is that the really successful, productive and powerful organizations (and their negotiators) prefer to use the contribution criterion as the distributive key, whereas their less successful, less productive and less powerful colleagues have a preference for the equality criterion. There is always a degree of subjectivity involved but regardless of who chooses and applies the distributive key, it is important that they should first search for a common, shared point of departure. This allows the parties to create a consensus for any further negotiations that may be necessary and provides a reference standard against which future developments can be tested.[34]

The following episode occurred at the Law of the Sea Conference.[35] At a certain moment, India – as a representative of the developing countries – put forward a proposal that deep-sea mining companies should pay an initial drilling fee for every mine they wished to open. The Indians suggested a fee of 60 million dollars per mine. This was rejected out of hand by the United States, who could see no reason why any fee should be payable. Both sides tried to convince the others that they were right, but without success – until someone discovered that the Massachusetts Institute of Technology (MIT) had constructed a model which could simulate the financial consequences of the proposed drilling fee. Both the Indians and the Americans accepted this model as a reasonable criterion.

And what exactly did this model reveal? The first five years of a mine are loss-making. If you were to add to this a very high starting cost, deep-sea mining would become uneconomical – which would be to no one's benefit. For this reason, the Indians agreed to look at their proposal again. The model showed that a more reasonable drilling fee was a realistic option, and this in turn persuaded the Americans to think again.

By using the MIT model as an external standard it was possible to free the negotiators from a stalemate situation and set them on a path towards a possible agreement: a solution that was both acceptable for the mining companies and brought sufficient income for the developing countries. This strengthened the understanding between the negotiators and made it more likely that the agreement would stand the test of time.

TIPS AND TRICKS

Key 3 offers you something extra: a number of simple, practical tips and tricks that can come in very handy during any negotiating situation. One of these tricks is an absolute classic, and is regarded by many as *the* way to divide up the negotiating cake: let one side cut the cake and let the other side choose its pieces. You will usually get a fair and reasonable division. This tactic proved to be of great value at the Law of the Sea Conference.

At a certain point, the negotiators had to share out the different prospective mine locations. 50% needed to be allocated to private mining companies and the other 50% to Enterprise, the mining organization of the United Nations. Most of the private mining companies come from rich countries that have the best technological know-how. The poor countries feared that Enterprise would lose out in the division.

Then someone came up with a surprise solution. Each private mining company would propose two possible mine locations to Enterprise. Enterprise would then have first choice of the two locations, with the other allocated to the private company. Because the private company could not know in advance which of the two locations it would get, it was 'forced' to offer Enterprise a choice of two promising sites. In this way, the negotiators allowed the superior expertise of the private companies to be used for the benefit of both sides.

Sometimes it is possible and advisable to first negotiate a set of arrangements, before deciding the role each party will play in those arrangements. For example, in divorce situations it is often better to first decide what practical measures need to be taken to ensure the proper care and development of the children, and only then to agree who is best suited to implement those measures. Moreover, this kind of distributive trick can be used in a wide variety of situations. For example, when distributing an inheritance it may be a good idea to let the beneficiaries draw lots to see who goes first or else allow each of them to choose an item in turn, which they can then exchange with each other afterwards (if they want to). Or they can use the services of an agreed arbitrator.

YOUR CONCESSION STRATEGY

'LIFE CANNOT SUBSIST IN SOCIETY BUT BY RECIPROCAL CONCESSIONS.'

(Samuel Johnson)

Our typical negotiating motto is: "Make as few concessions as possible." We often measure our results by the number of concessions we are required to make. Having said this, concessions can sometimes be a good investment because they trigger the reciprocity mechanism. There is no culture in the world where children are not taught that if they receive something, they must give something back in return.

Robert Cialdini, an expert in social influencing, has given us a clever example. On his way home one evening, a boy scout asked him to buy a 10 dollar ticket to attend a performance. Cialdini politely refused, whereupon the boy instantly asked: "So what about buying a bar of chocolate for 3 dollars, just to show your support?" Before he knew it, Cialdini had bought the chocolate, even though he never eats the stuff![36] The concession made by the boy – moving down from a major demand (10 dollars) to a minor demand (3 dollars) – triggered the reciprocity mechanism. Although we do not really like to be given no for an answer, the moment that follows conceals considerable potential for exercising influence.

Concessions have most impact if you can personalize them, if you can relate them directly to an interest of the other party. In the Conway case, for example, Smith might suggest setting up an advisory council in which he offers Conway a seat. It is self-evident that it is best to make a concession that is important for the other person and then in exchange ask for a concession that is important for you. In this way, you never lose sight of your lowest limit and the lower limit of your negotiating partner.

An NQ®-er does not make concessions randomly. He uses them consciously as a tool. He leaves nothing to chance or to the other person. He tries to plan the proposals and counter-proposals, so that they work to his advantage. In this respect, registration is an important factor. In the heat of negotiation, it is essential to know how many concessions you have made, what their scope was, and how many concessions the other person has made in return. The best way to do this is to simply note down the details of the concessions made by both sides. This will at any given moment allow you to see how far apart you still are or, conversely, how close an agreement might be. Many people get carried away by the intensity of the negotiation process to such an extent that they can no longer rationally analyze the concessions they have made. This can lead to various problems. (1) They make concessions too quickly, before they have even examined interests. (2) They make concessions but fail to realize that the other party is not making concessions in return. (3) They make concessions that are too big, so that the other party becomes suspicious or thinks that they are being too greedy.

The NQ®-er works more strategically and more carefully, and ensures that his concessions are logically developed. If Conway begins with an asking price of 60 million, but then drops this to 55 million without any apparent reason, this will have a counter-productive effect. It suggests that the first price was simply an attempt to get the other party to pay over the odds. If, however, the price reduction is linked to, for example, an agreement on Smith's part to pay in cash, the concession has a logical basis and will be accepted as reasonable.

The NQ®-er also knows that it is important for both sides to appreciate the concessions that are made. Negotiators often fall prey to reactive devaluation: they only want the things that they don't have or can't get. What they already possess or what they acquire in the course of the negotiations immediately decreases in value as soon as they get it.

From a psychological perspective, it is also worth noting that the number of concessions is more important than the weight of those concessions. It is therefore wiser to move step by step in the direction of your negotiating partner's demands, rather than trying to get there in a single giant leap.

With key 3 to a higher NQ®, you know that...

... you can protect yourself against hard and devious negotiators by daring to aim high and by sticking to your lowest limit, come what may. You will have a carefully defined BATNA to cover your back. Self-censure and fear of taking risks are neither a good WIN-WIN combination nor a way to achieve your goals or aspirations. In contrast, your BATNA is a powerful instrument: it gives you a negotiating position, helps you to guard against commitment escalation and boosts your SELF-CONFIDENCE.

Dividing the cake is an essential part of the negotiation process. Key 3 helps you to make the switch from value-creation to VALUE-CLAIMING, so that you can take home your share of the added value. External criteria with OBJECTIVE STANDARDS and a good concession strategy can help you to achieve this in a CONSTRUCTIVE and ASSERTIVE manner. If you need to make concessions, first identify and protect your core priorities, but be flexible on aspects that are less crucial to your interests. Concessions can be an excellent investment. Whatever else you do, make sure that you don't put your negotiating relationship at risk unnecessarily and also pay close ATTENTION TO DETAIL in this phase.

In order to bring your negotiations to the best possible conclusion, including the best possible share of the added value, you can employ the following tips:

- Don't be afraid to make serious demands near the upper limit of the ZOPA.
- Set a clear lower limit, since this:
  - defines the least good deal that you are willing to accept;
  - tells you when the time has come to walk away from the negotiating table.
- Set a good BATNA, since this:
  - makes you aware of other alternatives outside the framework of the current negotiations;
  - makes you less dependent on the outcome of the negotiations;
  - ensures a better end result.
- Use EXTERNAL STANDARDS or points of reference to convince others and protect yourself. Examples include market prices, precedents, the law, equality of treatment, competing offers, costs and best practice.
- Carefully consider your CONCESSION STRATEGY. Make sure that you develop this strategy in a logical manner. Take small steps forward rather than giant leaps, and protect your priorities.

KEY 4: SET THE RULES OF THE GAME

NEGOTIATING – A GAME?

'A GOOD PLAN IS LIKE A ROAD MAP: IT SHOWS THE FINAL DESTINATION AND USUALLY THE BEST WAY TO GET THERE.'

(H. Stanley Judd)

The famous and notorious Prisoners' Dilemma works as follows.[37] Two criminals have both committed the same crime, but there is insufficient evidence to convict them. The police lock them up in different rooms, so that they cannot communicate with each other. The officer in charge promises a significant sentence reduction to the first one who provides fresh information (in other words: squeals on his mate). If one confesses and the other one keeps silent, the snitch goes free and his partner will get 20 years. If they both confess, they both get five years. If neither confesses, they both go free, because of a lack of evidence.

	I CONFESS	**I KEEP SILENT**
HE CONFESSES	I GET A FIVE YEAR JAIL SENTENCE / HE GETS A FIVE YEAR JAIL SENTENCE.	I GET A 20 YEAR JAIL SENTENCE / HE GOES FREE.
HE KEEPS SILENT	I GO FREE / HE GETS A 20 YEAR JAIL SENTENCE.	I GO FREE / HE GOES FREE.

Because neither of them knows what the other one is going to do, they both confess. Why? Because if one keeps silent, he risks going to prison for 20 years, if his partner doesn't do the same. Both criminals are placed in a position where they are almost forced to choose the option they don't want. They are trapped by their own distrust. Or to put it in negotiating terms: they are a long way away from win-win.

The Prisoners' Dilemma is the best known example of game theory. With the help of this mathematical theory, we can analyze the strategic behaviour of decision-makers and negotiators (the 'players') and the way in which their actions influence each other. The choice of player A for a particular strategy – that must lead to the most beneficial outcome from his point of view – is based on his assessment of what the other player will do. And of course, player B does exactly the same.

An important assumption in game theory is that people are rational, that their interests and objectives are determined by the circumstances of the situation and, last but not least, that the rules of the game are fixed. Game theory, which is also widely used in the field of economics, is a technique to predict outcome on the basis of the interaction between decision-makers.

Another well-known game theory example is the game of 'chicken', where the objective is to be the last person to give up or admit something. There is a scene in the film classic *Rebel Without a Cause* (1955), in which two 'rebels', Jim (James Dean) and Buzz (Corey Allen), drive a car at full speed towards a precipice. The first one who jumps from the car before it crashes into the abyss is the 'chicken', and therefore loses. In the film, this 'game' has fatal consequences for Buzz, who leaves the car too late and plunges to his death. This is a key characteristic of the 'chicken' game. If no one gives up, the outcome will be bad for everyone.

Game theory is normative: it determines the best way to act in a specific situation. We have already seen that the utility function of people is often far from clear or objective – the positions taken by negotiators initially say nothing about their real interests and are often little more than a subjective decision to solve a particular problem in a particular manner (see Key 1).

But are the rules of the game fixed? Should you allow your own game to be determined by the way your opponent plays his game? Or can you change the rules of the game, so that they better work to your advantage? How can you make sure that you are playing the right game? Key 4 will show you the way. Key 4 is the key that will help you to steer the process and as such set the rules for the negotiating game. This process key unlocks an often forgotten source of negotiating strength: the value of taking the strategic lead in the negotiations. Key 4 not only helps you to do things the right way, but also to do the right things. To make this possible, it is necessary to 'zoom out' so that you can take a bird's-eye view of the situation.

Key 4 unlocks your strategic negotiating leadership at two different levels:

> AT THE NEGOTIATING TABLE, by ensuring that you use the keys in the right manner and the right moment, so that you play your own game and not the game that your negotiating partner wants you to play. In this way, you can guarantee that the RULES OF THE GAME are as good as they can be for the use of keys 1, 2 and 3.

> AWAY FROM THE NEGOTIATING TABLE, by enabling you to find out how you can determine the nature of the NEGOTIATING GAME, so that it best reflects your own interests. If you just passively take a seat at the existing negotiating table, you leave a large amount of potential unused. In contrast, if you use Key 4 to shape the architecture and set-up of the negotiations you can unlock a new zone of influence.

THE IMPORTANCE OF THE PROCESS

Until now, we have been largely concerned with *what* we want to negotiate: a good price for the take-over of a production company, the share of an orange, an acceptable border between Israel and Egypt...

Moving away from fixed positions and towards greater value creation was the central factor.

But *how* you negotiate can be just as important to the final outcome. The negotiating process and negotiating strategy – the rules of the negotiating game – offer you a wealth of new possibilities to exert influence.

Actually, the process also has an intrinsic value. People can sometimes get what they want but still be dissatisfied with the outcome, because of the way the process worked. The literature relating to procedural fairness shows the importance of the process not only in resolving conflicts, but also in providing satisfaction with the actual results achieved. For example, the judge in a court case may pronounce 100% in your favour, but you can still feel unhappy afterwards if you did not get the chance to say the things you wanted to say.[38] In other words, if you want to reach a win-win situation where both parties can feel that they have won, you need to steer the process with great skill and care. Using your keys at the right moment – before, during and after the negotiations – is essential in this respect.

AT THE NEGOTIATING TABLE: THE PROCESS AND THE RULES OF THE GAME

> Sophie wants to be promoted to the position of head nurse in the accident and emergency (A&E) department, a position that will soon be vacant. She has requested a conversation with Christine, the head doctor in A&E, and has carefully chosen a moment when she knows Christine cannot be called away. She greets the doctor cordially, asking about her recent sailing trip and how things are going with her daughter, who is currently studying at Harvard. She also says something about her own children. Sophie then frames the conversation by stating that she would like to discuss her future career perspectives.

Sophie and Christine are here playing out the *greeting phase* of the negotiations. You 'feel out' your negotiating partner, testing their reactions, setting the tone for the discussions, anchoring your style (cooperative or otherwise), exchanging pleasantries. This phase is important, since it helps you to build up or strengthen the negotiating relationship. In the West, we sometimes cut corners with this phase of the process. After all, time is money! But in many other cultures this is a crucial – perhaps the most crucial – phase, with an extensive ritual to which considerable time needs to be devoted.

If we devote attention to this phase, it is often with the intention of getting in the other person's good books. We suddenly pretend that we have become fascinated by sailing or would love to know all about Harvard. Often, however, this happens at the expense of finding out more about our common negotiating interests. It is far more important to focus on what you really appreciate in the other person than to try and make yourself popular with flattery. What do you admire about the other person? What do you like about them? '*It is not about making them like you, but about making sure you like them*'.[39] Because if people feel that you genuinely appreciate them for what they are, this is the best way to develop the trust that you need. Only then do you have authentic contact, and this is much stronger than mere pretence. We have already stressed the importance of this negotiating relationship (see the introduction). Key 4 will teach you that your best tactic during the greeting phase is to invest in a good understanding and in building up mutual confidence in each other – in this way, you will ensure that the rules of the game encourage NQ®-behaviour right from the very beginning.

Next comes the *exploration phase*. We continue to try and establish good relations with our negotiating partner but we now move on to content-related matters. This is the point at which Sophie's desire for promotion is brought into the open and put on the negotiating table.

Remember that the first steps you take, the first impression you make, can be crucial: this is how you anchor the style of your interaction with the other person. Once set, it is very difficult to change. Our process key tells us that this is now the moment to use Key 1.

Sophie does this by gradually nudging the conversation towards underlying interests. She enquires tentatively about Christine's interests and tries to shed some light on her own. They soon discover that they have a number of common and complementary interests. They discuss their motives and ideas, as well as their ambitions for the department. They are both enthusiastic about the possibility that Sophie will be given the head nurse's job. At this point, however, Christine puts additional job demands and conditions on the table. As a result of a planned restructuring, things will be harder in the department than ever before. Sophie will need to work more flexibly than in the past. Except when she is ill or on leave, she must be on call at all times, even during the night. And she must be able to get to the hospital within a reasonable period of time. Working overtime is a given, but will not always be compensated in full. Moreover, the composition of the A&E teams will change regularly and she cannot always expect cooperation.

If a team is short-staffed, Sophie will have to fill the gap at short notice and for as long as it takes. These new demands are too much for Sophie: she was hoping to negotiate on the basis of the existing conditions.

They have now arrived in the *resistance phase*. This phase has a strong pulling power. The more skilfully you can apply Key 1, the less resistance you are likely to encounter. This is also the phase in which positions that are not translated into interests will gradually come to be seen as irreconcilable problems – and will therefore encourage further resistance. If you do not use Key 1 at this point, the negotiations will quickly degenerate into an all too familiar tug-of-war. In the above situation, Christine has switched too brusquely from an incomplete exploration of interests to a series of value demands (Key 3). She omits Key 2 altogether, which suggests that for her the exploration of interests was just a formality and that the time has now come to get down to the real nitty-gritty.

Does this sound familiar? Much the same thing happened during the discussions between Conway and Smith. After a brief greeting phase, they began a constructive conversation about underlying interests, so that the prospect of a successful take-over soon became a very real one. But their interests were not used for value creation, so that they quickly found themselves in the resistance phase.

The NQ®-er knows that the real art is to take the barbs out of the negotiations – the obstacles that are preventing one of the parties from moving forward and which therefore do not represent promising material for step 2: the creation of added value. These stumbling blocks are nothing more or less than our entrenched positions and so we need to approach them in the manner we have already discussed. Do not begin by defending yourself, but attempt to explore, clarify, paraphrase and check off the concerns of the other person. Instead of becoming involved in a cycle of bid and counter-bid, try instead to employ the tactics of Key 1. This should get you out of a stalemate position. Only then will you be ready to make a counter-proposal or put forward a possible solution. The resistance phase often leads to an impasse or even the complete breakdown of the negotiations.

> Fortunately, Sophie and Christine manage to work their way through this difficult phase. They examine the interests behind Christine's position and Sophie's reluctance. Why is more flexibility such an important criterion for promotion? Is the work situation in A&E really so unpredictable? Realistically, how often is the head nurse likely to be called up in the middle of the night? Is there no

possibility to rewrite other job descriptions, so that the burden of irregular hours is more evenly shared?

In this manner, they arrive at the *transforming phase*. Our NQ®-er knows that this is the moment when Key 2 needs to be used in conjunction with Key 4, putting all different kinds of possible options on the negotiating table and maximising the opportunities to reach creative, value-enhancing solutions. What about transport? Sophie says that she needs to collect her children from day care each day. But she doesn't have a car. Until now she has always managed with public transport. The child-minders are prepared to wait until she arrives, but this means that she has to pay a bit extra. Christine suggests that part of her salary increase as head nurse could be used to provide a company car. She could also use the hospital's own nursery, which opens earlier and closes later than most external day care centres. And if there are still occasions on which she needs to pay for private child care, her higher salary should also help to cover these costs. Or perhaps the head nurse position is suitable for job sharing? The new head nurse appointment might be an ideal opportunity to restructure the job content, making it more strategic and less hands-on. Christine is particularly enthusiastic about this last idea. As head of the A&E department, she spends too much of her valuable time discussing the implementation of the new quality norms and the regional redistribution of hospital functions. As a result, she is away from her department quite often and in danger of losing touch with her patients and her staff. It would be ideal if Sophie could take over a number of these external tasks. Not job sharing, exactly, but a redistribution of tasks between the doctor and her senior nurse. It is an option that seems to have clear benefits for them both.

Sophie and Christine carefully weigh up the pros and cons. This is the beginning of the *evaluation phase*. Sophie starts by making use of Key 3.

> Sophie examines whether or not her pay increase will be sufficient to farm out a number of other domestic tasks, so that working overtime is not a problem. She also asks for proper remuneration for her overtime and for priority in the use of the hospital's limited day care facilities. Together, they evaluate all the options and the added value they can create. They gradually move in the direction of a final outcome that seems positive for both sides. But it doesn't always work this way. Even at this late stage things can still go wrong. Incorrect or insufficient application of one of the four keys can still throw the negotiations back into the resistance phase.

Fortunately, this does not happen with Sophie and Christine. In the *closure phase* they reach a final agreement. They discuss the deal, examine the details one by one, prepare a summary and agree on the next steps to be taken. The correct use of Key 4 implies that this is the moment when you must take particular care before you finally shake hands on the deal – redistributing the cake afterwards is infinitely more difficult. Does the deal really satisfy the interests you identified with Key 1? Does it give you enough of the added value you helped to create with Key 2? Are you above the lowest limit that you set with Key 3? Have you achieved a fair and equitable sharing of the cake? Check to make sure that you have not overlooked any points of importance and that the agreement can be implemented without the need for any further amendment.

As all the above shows, it is essential to know when you should use each key and how you can steer the process AT THE NEGOTIATING TABLE. The person who is capable of controlling this process is in a strong position to determine the direction the negotiations will take. He will set the rules of the game, often proactively. This means that he will set the tone for the discussions and will thereby avoid the need to simply respond to the challenges thrown down by the other side.

NQ®-ers use Key 4 to effectively employ their knowledge of the process phase to steer the process and make full strategic use of the other keys. But real NQ®-ers also know that the correct use of Key 4 will allow them to go even further. It makes them aware of another hidden – yet very powerful – source of negotiating influence. They understand the need to control the negotiating situation not only at the negotiating table, but also AWAY FROM THE NEGOTIATING TABLE. In this way, they not only determine the rules of the game, but also the game itself: the architecture of the negotiations. Playing the game to the best of your ability is fine, but if you can actually decide what game you and your negotiating partners are playing, this strengthens your position immeasurably.

AWAY FROM THE NEGOTIATING TABLE: DETERMINING THE GAME

We all know that we should prepare thoroughly for negotiations and we all know that this doesn't always happen. This is a serious mistake. Correct preparation of the four keys is a crucial factor in determining the level of effectiveness with which you can employ them.

At the same time, the NQ®-er knows that key 4 opens a second door to negotiating leadership. The NQ®-er will not only prepare himself in terms of the existing negotiations, a game whose shape and rules have already been set. He will also investigate how it may be possible to give the game a different shape and a new set of rules: his rules.

Let us step back in time to the year 1995. The OECD (Organisation for Economic Cooperation and Development) set up negotiations to reach a Multilateral Investment Agreement. The agreement was necessary to ensure the liberalization and proper organization of foreign direct investment, which had risen from 25 billion dollars in 1973 to almost 350 billion dollars in 1995, a fourteen-fold increase with no proper framework for international cooperation. Government leaders as well as key business actors recognised the need for such a framework. Because the OECD zone accounted for 85% of all investments, it was decided that the organization was the right forum for negotiations.

It was assumed that the negotiations would be pretty straightforward: little more than the codification of an existing consensus. But the negotiators were overtaken by the course of history and something wholly unexpected happened.

In the 1990s, environmental and development NGO's had begun to demand increasing access to the closed negotiating world of trade and financial agreements. They became better organized internationally and began to force their way into areas that had previously been the exclusive preserve of the great investment institutions. More specifically, they zoomed in on the trend towards increasing globalization, which in their view equalled de-politicization and the right of the strongest.

A number of the NGO's became aware of the MIA negotiations and knocked at the door of the OECD. They wanted a place at the negotiating table and a say in setting the agenda, particularly on key social and environmental themes. Although there were already a number of trade union representatives at the negotiating table, the link between FDI and social-environmental concerns was still not properly made. FDI was simply seen as a good thing, full stop.

Because they were not being listened to, the NGO's decided to 'change the game'. They launched an anti-MIA campaign that portrayed the MIA as a vampire, sucking the lifeblood out of democracy around the world. The NGO's accused the OECD of conspiring with the giant multinationals and mobilized public opinion behind their cause. Soon the debate was taken up by the press and parliaments of many different countries. These actions heralded the birth of the anti-globalisation movement. (Tieleman, in preparation).

And the miracle occurred! The official negotiations gradually acquired a new and increasingly social-environmental dimension, as did the texts coming out of the meetings. It became inevitable that the OECD would be forced to invite the NGO's for discussions, but by then it was too late to turn back the clock. The genie had already escaped the bottle: the NGO's had become a player and had changed the agenda. But the distrust that had forced them to take this action meant that they were now no longer willing to negotiate. The anti-MIA campaign had found such resonance around the world that the coalition of NGO's emerged as the undisputed winner against the forces of financial and political consensus. Four years after their start, the OECD negotiations collapsed in failure.

Could the OECD have done anything else? Could they have used Key 4 differently? If you want to shape the game,[40] it is essential to think about who the right players are – the genuine stakeholders. This often seems easier than it really is. To get the right players to the table in this instance, the OECD as an NQ®-er should not only have looked at the past, but also to the future. They should have asked proactively who could and should have been involved in the process, and what COALITIONS might possibly be formed. If they had done this, the OECD negotiators might have realised sooner that while the NGO's were not necessarily a negotiating partner, they were certainly a stakeholder. This realization could have opened the door to a fruitful dialogue.

A good NQ®-er knows that it is always useful to involve the likely implementers of any agreement in the discussions. Conway and Smith were able to conclude an excellent agreement on the basis of the four keys. And thanks to their understanding of Key 4, they also knew that the successful translation of this agreement into practice was quite dependent on the extent to which they involved all the people likely to be directly affected by it. These implementers can best assess how feasible, realistic and costly particular options in the agreement might be. Moreover, this involvement also makes the implementers more motivated to carry out the terms of the agreement reached. As such, the added value created at the negotiating table is optimally translated into results. After all, you do not negotiate simply to conclude a paper agreement but to prompt concrete action.

You also need to ask yourself about your ideal AGENDA. What should be on it? Which subjects should you deal with first? Should you start with the most difficult themes or the easiest ones? Which themes can easily be linked to the negotiations and which ones are best avoided? How should you frame the different points on the agenda? This framing is crucial for the manner in which they will be dealt with. For example, the OECD should have asked whether its MIA negotiations were best framed in a financial dimension or in a social-environmental dimension. In other words, was the MIA a straightforward financial matter or were important societal forces also at play? The OECD should also have been more aware of the relevance of its negotiating framework and more willing to be flexible in its approach. The points on the agenda, their order of priority and their framing determine to a large extent what actually happens at the negotiating table and have a considerable impact on the selection of the relevant stakeholders. By framing the agenda points correctly, you can influence who actually sits at the negotiating table.

Which FORMAT should the OECD have chosen? The table at which you negotiate, its location and the format you use are all crucial matters, which allow you to exert influence on the negotiating process. Do you approach the other negotiating parties simultaneously or one at a time? Do you negotiate behind closed doors or do you allow the general public, perhaps even the press, into your negotiations? The OECD clearly thought very little about these matters. They could – and should – have been much more active in their use of formal and informal negotiating space to create both a public and a closed negotiating area. This tactic has been used to good effect in many more recent top-level international negotiations in the trade and finance fields, not only by the OECD but also by the World Trade Organization and the United Nations.

The OECD should also have thought about the best way to create the right EXPECTATIONS and the best BATNAS, both for itself and for the other partners. An NQ®-er exerts influence, both formally and informally, guides and advises, mobilizes people, activates ideas and knows how to get things done. An NQ®-er uses strategies and processes without ever losing sight of the relationships. In this way, the NQ®-er becomes a shaper.

ARE YOU A FOLLOWER OR A SHAPER?

'NEGOTIATION INVOLVES MOVES AWAY FROM THE TABLE TO SET UP THE MOST PROMISING SITUATION ONCE YOU'RE AT THE TABLE.'

(M. Watkins)

Key 4 allows you to make best use of the negotiation strategy matrix reproduced in the following table[41] and to become a shaper, rather than a follower.

	FOLLOWER	SHAPER
AT THE NEGOTIATING TABLE	› ALLOWS THE RULES OF THE GAME TO BE DETERMINED BY THE CIRCUMSTANCES AND THE OPPOSING PARTY; › IS NOT FAMILIAR WITH THE DIFFERENT NEGOTIATION PHASES OR THE WAY THE NEGOTIATING PROCESS DEVELOPS; › DOES NOT KNOW HOW OR WHEN TO USE KEYS 1, 2 AND 3.	› SETS THE RULES OF THE GAME AND MAXIMIZES THE OPPORTUNITIES FOR VALUE CREATION; › IS FAMILIAR WITH THE DIFFERENT NEGOTIATION PHASES OR THE WAY THE NEGOTIATING PROCESS DEVELOPS; › USES KEYS 1, 2 AND 3 TO STEER THE PROCESS AND GUIDE IT IN THE PREFERRED DIRECTION.
AWAY FROM THE NEGOTIATING TABLE	› ALLOWS THE CIRCUMSTANCES AND THE OPPOSING PARTY TO DECIDE THE TYPE OF NEGOTIATING GAME THAT WILL BE PLAYED; › TAKES PLACE AT THE NEGOTIATING TABLE WITHOUT TOO MUCH THOUGHT AND ACCEPTS THE ARCHITECTURE OF THE NEGOTIATIONS AS IT IS. › PAYS LITTLE ATTENTION TO PREPARATION AND IMPLEMENTATION.	› DETERMINES THE GAME THAT EVERYONE WILL PLAY; › MAKES UNILATERAL CHANGES TO THE ARCHITECTURE OF THE NEGOTIATING TABLE (THE PARTICIPATING STAKEHOLDERS, COALITIONS, THE AGENDA, DEADLINES AND OTHER IMPORTANT ELEMENTS); › RECOGNISES THAT PREPARATION AND FOLLOW-UP ARE INTEGRAL PARTS OF THE NEGOTIATIONS.

A follower does not take key matters into his own hands. He allows the rules of the game and even the game itself to be decided by others and by the circumstances of the situation. He has a poor understanding of the different phases of the negotiations and the keys that should be used to maximize his benefit from each of those different phases. He is happy to take part in the negotiating game that others have prepared for him.

In contrast, the shaper takes circumstances by the scruff of the neck and moulds them to suit his own purposes. He determines the rules of the game, navigating skilfully through the different phases of the negotiations with the help of the four keys. He persuades others to play the game that he wants to play, and tells them how that game both looks and works.

By shaping the game away from the negotiating table, we can influence the game played at the negotiation table. These parallel games 'at the negotiating table' and 'away from the negotiating table' are inextricably but not always chronologically linked to each other. As a leader or shaper we can exert considerable influence on them. If the results at the negotiating table are currently disappointing, you can zoom out to see how the rules of the game can be changed to your advantage – perhaps by inviting a new conversation partner or ditching a particular point on the agenda and creating room for another. Changing the agenda also has an impact on coalition-forming. It can bond or cause coalitions to fall apart. Game-shaping negotiations therefore involve much more than straightforward face-to-face interaction.

Key 4 allows you to switch from tactics to strategy and from the short term to the long term. As we have already mentioned, most negotiations are not 'one-off' events but part of a longer process, which means that you will be confronted with the same negotiating partners time after time – either directly or through your reputation. By adding Key 4 to your perspective you add a new dimension, just as you would when looking with two eyes rather than just one. Instead of a flat world, you suddenly see it in all its complexity.

If the situation at the negotiating table is not looking promising, the NQ®-er does not try to get his own way by intimidating, as a win-lose negotiator would. He will first try to change things away from the negotiating table. In this way, he can reset the table, becoming the architect of a new game through his skilled use of Key 4. To do this, he will ask himself a number of questions:[42]

> How can we organize ourselves to influence the process?
> Who are the most important stakeholders?
> Which coalitions offer interesting possibilities? Which should we avoid?
> Ideally, what do we want the agenda to look like?
> Which are the most promising framing strategies? How do we expect the other parties to frame the different subjects for negotiation?
> How are these negotiations linked to other negotiations? What links do we want to make? What links do we want to avoid?
> Which forum offers the best opportunities to lead and steer the negotiations to our advantage?

This is how the NQ®-er will not only do things the right way, but will also do the right things.

With key 4 to a higher NQ, you know that...

.... the negotiating PROCESS is just as important as the final objective. The NQ®-er knows that key 4 makes it possible to determine both the rules of the game AT THE NEGOTIATING TABLE and the game itself AWAY FROM THE NEGOTIATING TABLE. He is familiar with the different phases of the process and exploits these skilfully and with ease, in order to steer the negotiations in the direction of greater value creation and optimal results. He also understands that the process neither begins nor ends with face-to-face interaction. As a true shaper, he moulds the architecture of the negotiations.

Before he takes his place at the negotiating table, he has already investigated and influenced the entire set-up. He wants to be sure that all the right parties are approached in the right order, so that the right subjects can be dealt with in the right place at the right time. He approaches matters STRATEGICALLY and does much more than simply play the game. He recreates the range and the possibilities of the negotiations. He also pays sufficient attention to the problems of implementation. He never stops negotiating prematurely and he always involves the likely implementers in the final deal. He is proactive, has a bird's eye perspective, dares to take the lead and is ready to dictate the game. In short, the smart negotiator is a GAME ARCHITECT, from the planning phase right through to implementation.

The NQ®-er has the following advice:

- Do not focus exclusively on the WHAT of the negotiations, but also on the HOW.
- Manage the negotiation process and the negotiating strategy as this offers invaluable possibilities for influence.
- Remember that the process works at two different levels: at the negotiating table and away from the negotiating table.
- Be a shaper, not a follower.
- Become thoroughly familiar with the negotiating phases that take place at the negotiating table and with the pitfalls that you may encounter, so that you can determine the right rules of the game for each phase.
- Remember that what happens away from the negotiating table is just as important as what happens at the table itself.

2

FROM NQ® TO CORPORATE NQ®

Is it possible to save 37 million dollars simply by concluding a corporate agreement with a strategic negotiating approach? A company that introduced such an approach just a few years ago, with specific attention for the preparation and planning elements, did indeed achieve this incredible result. Another company put it this way: "If we would just pick up all the money we leave needlessly lying around, it would amount to tens, if not hundreds, of millions."

And what to make of the dramatic fall in negotiating time from 12-18 months to less than eight weeks for 75% of all complex projects with a budget greater than five million dollars? Can this really be achieved just by introducing a proper negotiating infrastructure? You bet it can!

These are real examples from a large-scale benchmark study[43] of the 'negotiation maturity' of the world's largest companies – including Microsoft, Sara Lee, TNT, Siemens, BP, General Motors and Alcatel-Lucent. With convincing figures, this study documents the advantages of working with a structured negotiating approach at company level, or raising the level of corporate negotiating skill or intelligence. As an extension of the NQ® concept, the use of negotiation intelligence at organizational level is here referred to as Corporate NQ®.

The top 25 companies that scored highest on the negotiating maturity scale saw their profits rise by 42.5% between 2007 and 2008. During that same period the net profit of the Global 2000 (the world's leading 2,000 companies, according to *Forbes Magazine*) fell by 30.9%. For companies that failed to use structured negotiating processes, the results were even worse: an average fall in profits of 63.3%.

How exactly does Corporate NQ® give added competitive strength and vitality to the companies that use it? With the arrival of more complex business models, the creation of alliances in ever-bigger chains, increasing international competition, growing prosperity, specialized market segments, the rise of the zapping consumer and the development of transparent markets, the smartest among companies are devoting more and more time to the care and maintenance of sustainable relations and agreements with their most important stakeholders and business partners.

WORKING TOGETHER FOR PROFIT

'EVERY COMPANY TODAY EXISTS IN A COMPLEX WEB OF RELATIONSHIPS, AND THE SHAPE OF THAT WEB IS FORMED, ONE THREAD AT A TIME, THROUGH NEGOTIATIONS.'

(Danny Ertel)

As we already suggested in our introduction, we all negotiate all the time – at home, at school, in the digital marketplace, in politics... So do companies and organizations. Negotiation is one of their vital core activities, spanning from tens to thousands of separate negotiations each year depending on the size of the company and its negotiating level.

These negotiations take place both at micro level (for example, between colleagues) and macro level (strategic decisions), both internally and externally. In a modern management structure much more internal negotiation takes place than did in the past (see introduction), but the importance of external negotiations is also on the increase. After all, the future of successful companies is to be found in 'capacity building', partnerships and alliances. Strategic collaboration with partners is an effective and perhaps even essential condition for first consolidating and then improving your position in the market. More than 35% of stock market value in Europe and the United States in 2002 was generated by alliances – 'the organizational form of the knowledge economy'.[44] Alliances between companies, or the network of collaborating partners in which they are embedded, increasingly determine the competitive strength of organizations. The purposes of such alliances are: (1) increased efficiency – economies of scale and scope; (2) access to new markets or market segments; (3) a greater ability to meet specific customer demands; (4) spreading out innovation risk; (5) limiting or avoiding competition (De Man, 2006).

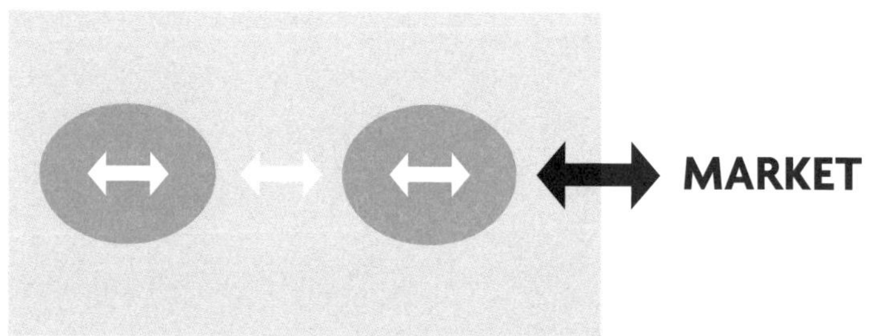

Collaborative partners negotiate internally, with each other and with the market to improve their position.

An example of a very successful alliance is the opportunistic collaboration between Philips and Sara Lee/Douwe Egberts (Senseo). Together, they created a new coffee concept and launched it onto the market. Equally well-known and successful are the partnerships involving Mercedes Benz and Swatch (Smart) and Heineken and Krups (Beertender). The IT-sector has seen an explosion of such collaborative ventures and take-overs in recent years. This is largely the result of ever-increasing competition and the rapid pace of innovation. As a result, companies are almost forced to seek each other's help. Hardware and software manufacturers, service developers and resellers need to cooperate if they hope to meet constantly changing consumer demand and remain competitive. Examples of such ventures included Microsoft and Nokia (Windows Phone), Google and HTC (Google phone), Apple and telecom-providers Mobistar and T-Mobile (who for some time had the exclusive rights to selling the iPhone in Belgium and Holland/Germany respectively). For much the same reasons, take-overs are still common in the sector – consider Microsoft's absorption of Skype. There have also been dozens of innovations during the past few years that have been developed by linking parallel market segments, such as the portable clock with GPS, created by TomTom and Nike. All these examples are different types of capacity building which demand a high degree of NQ® at company level.

The greater the interlocking with or dependence on chain partners or other external parties becomes, the greater the need for carefully negotiated collaborative agreements becomes as well. Do these complex structures necessarily mean that you will lose time and money? No, not at all. Productive friction – the creative tension that results from negotiation and collaboration both within the company and beyond – can often stimulate organizations to discover innovations and methods of working that accelerate capability building.[45] However, productive friction is a process that needs to be promoted and steered with care or it may turn into non-productive friction. This can lead to misunderstandings, dead-end streets and damaged relationships. To allow productive friction to blossom, you must focus on shared interests. Above all, you must ensure that your company is a Corporate NQ® company.

NEGOTIATING THE WALL STREET WAY?

The total of the outcomes of all micro- and macro-level corporate negotiations determine the success, strength and sustainability of organizations. In other words: negotiation has a significant effect on the bottom line. In view of the prevailing commercial-economic context (see above), this effect will only increase. It offers an interesting business opportunity. As opposed to other critical commercial processes, such as purchasing, logistics, outsourcing, legal, HRM and finance, the strategic use of negotiation at company level is still the monopoly of a few *front runners*. Only about 20% of leading companies have so far initiated measures to build up their Corporate NQ®.[46]

For Corporate NQ®, the negotiating skills of the individual negotiators are, of course, a *sine qua non.* Even so, developing these alone is not enough. Corporate NQ® is more than the sum total of the company's individual NQ®-ers. In addition to the four keys that the NQ®-ers have at their disposal, the organizational context within which they negotiate is also of crucial importance for the manner in which these keys can actually be used. After all, the first question an individual negotiator must always ask himself is this: in what framework am I negotiating?

The importance of the negotiating context is beautifully illustrated by the following experiment:

Two groups were assembled. One group was told that they were going to play the Community Game. The other group was told that they were going to play the Wall Street Game. The two games are actually identical (except for the name) but with one important exception: the outcome. In the Community Game 70% of the test subjects collaborate and engage in a win-win scenario. In the Wall Street Game the figures are reversed: to start with, only 30% of the participants work together and they will stop if they cannot persuade the other 70% to join in. The participants act win-lose and eventually oriented.[47]

The outcome of the experiment showed the importance of context and framing. The negotiating framework affected no less than 40% of the people taking part in the experiment. The participants who thought that they were operating in a framework that rewarded self-interest operated accordingly. The participants who thought that they were operating in a win-win environment were much more willing to demonstrate pro-social behaviour. Judged by descriptions of people who knew the participants in daily life, the influence of the framework appeared to affect the participants more strongly than their own personal characteristics. People who were seen as selfish were more inclined to behave selflessly in the first group, while people who were seen as collaborative were more likely to become deliberately uncooperative in the context of the Wall Street Game.

Context matters. But what does this mean for your company? Do you negotiate in a Wall Street context or in a Community context? As a company director, a manager or even as an ordinary member of staff, you play an active role in setting the negotiation framework. Which framework should you offer as a manager? How can you influence the people who work for you? In short, how can you create the right conditions, so that you can evolve from NQ® to Corporate NQ®?

A CORPORATE NQ® MENTALITY

Many companies fail to realize that they do have a choice – and so they organize for Wall Street. Otherwise, they believe, people will only abuse the system: human nature may be more cooperative than we sometimes think (see introduction), but when it comes to business, people will not be willing to cooperate without the necessary carrots and sticks (rewards and punishments). But is this true?

Do you know the story of the *Tragedy of the Commons*? A group of farmers shared a piece of land on which they were allowed to graze their cattle without restrictions. The farmers all kept putting more and more cattle on the land, until all the grass was eaten away, so that there was nothing left for anyone. No one was prepared to moderate his behaviour. No one was prepared to reduce his number of cattle in relation to his neighbours, who would only use the free space to put on more cattle of their own, so that all the grass would still be eaten. The conclusion is clear: without rules and supervision, people as 'free riders' will seek to obtain the benefits of common resources, while hoping to avoid (or simply ignoring) the disadvantages. In this way, the common resources are quickly destroyed.[48]

However, even this 'free-rider' principle – one of the cornerstones of the philosophy of the rational, interest-driven players – has now become outdated and is increasingly seen as too one-dimensional. In 2009, Elinor Ostrom was awarded the Nobel Prize for Economics by showing that 'the commons' can be managed in a sustainable manner without the need to create some kind of Hobbesian 'Leviathan' – a draconian overseer. In Spain, for example, thousands of farmers have been negotiating with each other for centuries over access to water.[49] More modern examples include Wikipedia and TripAdvisor.

Are we, in fact, less selfish and more cooperative in our negotiating approach than we often think? If so, how can companies capitalise on this cooperative element?

The deep-rooted conviction that people negotiate on the basis of the strict profit-loss principles of self-interest is gradually being undermined from several different quarters (psychology, sociology, political science, experimental economy and biology). In his article 'The Unselfish Gene', Yochai Benkler[50] argues, for example, that one of the most striking achievements of evolution has been its ability to engender cooperation in an essentially competitive world. Benkler sees natural collaboration as a third key pillar of evolution, alongside mutation and natural selection. Is this correct?

Experiments testing cooperative behaviour show that a large minority behaves in an egotistical manner. But they also show that about half of all people demonstrate systematically cooperative behaviour – some of them conditionally (with people who are also friendly towards them), the rest unconditionally (even if this means they have to pay a price). The remaining group – about 20% – is unpredictable. Sometimes they cooperate and sometimes they don't. But in none of the experiments did a majority of people behave in a selfish manner.[51] This, of course, has huge consequences for every cooperative system and for every company. Do you design your company context to reflect the behaviour of the uncooperative 30% or the cooperative 70%? If you focus on the 30%, you will leave a large part of the human potential in your company unused. Moreover, if you choose to follow the egoists, you know in advance that the value creation foreseen through the use of Key 2 will be frustrated, so that a beneficial win-win situation becomes virtually impossible. In other words, you will be losing out twice.

For this reason, the opposite argument is gaining ground. Namely, that in addition to their natural desire to score, negotiators should also have a predisposition for cooperation. Companies should make much greater use of engagement, empowerment and intrinsic motivation.

The challenge now is for companies to change mental attitude, so that they can create a framework in which people can collaborate, negotiate on a win-win basis and make the most efficient use of the four negotiating keys. Why? Because well-motivated and highly skilled NQ®-ers feel most at home in an organization with a high Corporate NQ®.

To begin, we need to stop viewing negotiation in isolation. We must cease regarding it as an ad hoc process, in which the negotiators are lone wolves who may or may not be good at what they do. Instead, we need to look at negotiations at an organizational level.

A LONE WOLF NEVER WALKS ALONE

'TREATING NEGOTIATION COMPETENCE SOLELY AS A MATTER OF INDIVIDUAL SKILL-BUILDING IS A COSTLY MISTAKE.'

(Movius & Susskind)

> Bingo! Another big deal landed! John Brookman, who works in the fast-moving consumer goods (FMCG) sector, can always be relied upon to produce the very best purchasing results. An assertive soloist who knows all the rules and tricks of the game. This time it isn't so much that he has negotiated a super-low price, but that he has also secured excellent delivery conditions. The ability to deliver

quickly is a key determining factor in this line of business so if a certain product runs out, it has to be re-supplied within four hours. If not, Brookman's company can order the same product from another supplier who is able to deliver, passing on all costs to the regular supplier.

But Brookman's success doesn't always translate into success for his colleagues. Recent market research revealed that his company needs to do better in terms of customer-friendliness and added value for its services. In fact, in these areas the scores are so poor that the critical lowest level has almost been reached. Any further reduction in the quality of service provision could result in customers transferring their business to the company's direct competitor. This competitor also happens to be highly creative with state-of-the-art applications. Unfortunately, Jean-Luc is not all that bothered about customer relations: he is more concerned with the thought of all the money he is saving the company.

Last year the supplier had to accept a lower price. This year the delivery conditions have worsened. As a result, the supplier is no longer inclined to share his insights into the most recent market developments with Brookman's company. After all, the margin on their services has now dropped to an absolute minimum. The pleasure of doing business with each other also vanished long ago. Perhaps the time has come to shift the focus to other market partners who can offer more synergetic advantages – not only in terms of price, but also in ways that will allow the quality of the products to be guaranteed.

It is clear that the marketing department in Brookman's company is far from happy with his new contract. And much the same applies to product development and sales. The buyers might be getting all the glory, but everyone else is left to pick up the pieces – and they are getting sick of it.

A soloist, like Jean-Luc, has little time for others who cast doubt on his way of doing business, others who suggest that his results are affecting feasibility in other areas and who point to the delays resulting from the legal disputes that he constantly provokes.

"You get the best results behind closed doors," he argues. "Afterwards I tell everyone what I have achieved and no one can dispute that I have obtained the best possible results. They all know me by now!"

Indeed they do – and a lot of people, both inside and outside the company, are no longer happy about it...

If individual negotiators and negotiating objectives are not subject to and supported by an overarching negotiation strategy, their agreements can often be counter-productive from a strategic point of view. Brookman negotiated *situationally* instead of *institutionally*. This testifies to a lack of organizational sensitivity. He is insufficiently aware of the influence and impact of his decisions on the rest of his company.

Brookman is by no means an isolated case. Like many other negotiators, he sees each negotiation as an ad hoc event, a new trajectory that requires a new and specific approach. Departments or individuals like Brookman negotiate in a vacuum, isolated from the company's wider strategy and its overriding priorities.

As we have already seen above, organizations that opt for a different approach score consistently better.

A DIFFERENT WAY: NEGOTIATING AS AN ORGANIZATION

The Mexican bank Grupo Financiero Serfin has taken a number of steps in the direction of Corporate NQ®. During the currency crisis of the 1990s, many of the bank's customers found it difficult to keep up their loan repayment schedules. The bank reacted in the usual manner and arranged meetings with all its major debtors. The purpose was to discuss what percentage of the loan they could repay, in exchange for supplementary commitments. If necessary, the bank's negotiators threatened to take legal action.

Notwithstanding the recruitment of new staff and the provision of additional specialist training, Serfin found it impossible to improve the return on its lending portfolio. And so the bank decided to change course. It developed a negotiating structure for the whole organization. This contributed to a growing awareness amongst staff that negotiations were not just a series of different one-off events, but a constituent part of a continuing institutional process. The new infrastructure encouraged the bank's negotiators to develop new and innovative solutions, working in close consultation with the customers.[52]

Corporate NQ® implies a move towards approaching negotiations in a strategic, holistic and systematic way. A number of questions can help you on your way. Are your company's negotiations ad hoc, one-off events or is there an overarching strategy? Are you aware of and do you understand your company's negotiating leverage? Has an assessment been made of how and with whom synergetic advantages (in terms of innovation, competition and scale) can be obtained via negotiation? Who are the most important stakeholders in the long term? When and how can the company achieve competitive advantage through negotiation? What is the relationship between individual negotiating objectives and the wider company strategy and priorities? What measures have been taken to ensure the proper training and development of the company's negotiators? Are there indicators in place to evaluate the quality of negotiating practice and is this quality actively measured? Is knowledge acquired during the negotiating trajectory properly disseminated throughout the entire organization?

The nature of these questions shows that Corporate NQ® is not just about business, but about business *development*. This requires an integrated long-term vision and strategy that you must always take to and from the negotiating table. For this reason, it is vital that negotiation should become an organizational process, for which a specific policy should be drawn up.

The following figure illustrates a typical Corporate NQ® policy cycle.

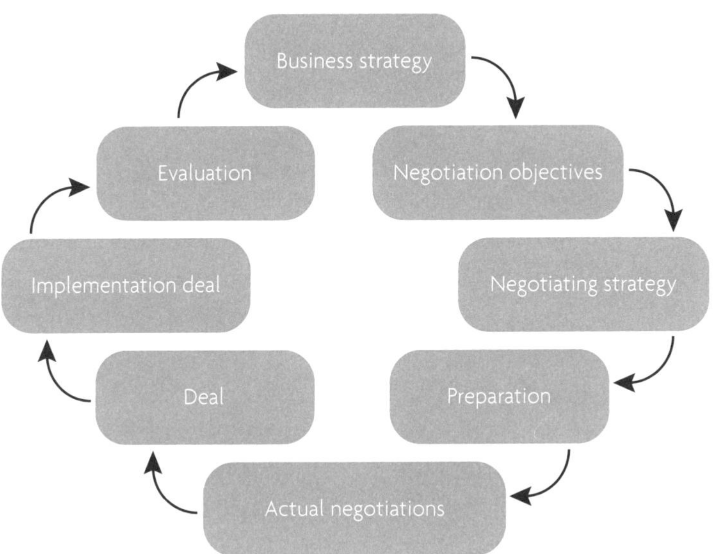

A powerful way of forcing negotiators to confront the realities of business development is to withhold their authority to negotiate until they have produced a solid negotiating plan, which is clearly linked to the company strategy (Huthwaite International/IACCM, 2009).

Once you start to think about negotiations organisationally instead of situationally, what is the best way to anchor a new negotiating infrastructure in the DNA of your organization in a manner that will guarantee you a high level of Corporate NQ®? The following section offers a number of useful guidelines, including examples from some front runners.

A CORPORATE NQ® INFRASTRUCTURE: SOME GUIDELINES

The right instruments and structures

A quarter of the benchmarked companies that are using formal aids to assist in the planning of negotiations have reported a significant change in results (see above – Huthwaite International/IACCM, 2009). The first step towards the development of a negotiating infrastructure at organizational level is setting up the right structures and instruments. This includes making tools available that can support the negotiators in their task.

From a structural perspective, this means that you should not only look at existing procedures and structures in terms of their possible contribution toward an increased Corporate NQ®, but also design new ones. In this respect, it is particularly important to think beyond 'silos'. Less than half the companies in the above-mentioned benchmark study have a system for cross-organizational collaboration – collaboration which covers the full range of silos, across the length and breadth of the company (Huthwaite International/IACCM, 2009). Cross-silo thinking is an essential aspect of Corporate NQ®. It is essential to develop joined-up solutions for your company's problems and objectives. There is no point in one department achieving its targets at the cost of another department's targets. Processes must be devised that take account of and integrate the targets of every department. In most cases, common objectives and real innovation can only be achieved through the genuine collaboration of all concerned.

This de-compartmentalization goes still further than breaking the boundaries between internal silos. As outlined above, in the current economic context it is increasingly necessary to search for partners *outside* your own organization. This is often the only way to achieve success. An alliance mindset implies the optimization of all your commercial processes, even if this takes you far beyond the boundaries of your own company.

At the same time, it is important to develop the necessary instruments. For example: (1) a tailor-made and flexible preparation process, including the necessary tools to plan the negotiations; (2) fixed procedures for choosing the members of your negotiating teams; (3) a priority plan at organizational level instead of at the level of individual agreements; (4) methods for linking clear and assessable negotiating objectives to broader company objectives; (5) the means to conduct a structural BATNA analysis or concession strategy; (6) a corporate specification for negotiations.[53] In this way, you will ensure that the whole company supports the process of value creation in the long term.

Facilitate and reward Corporate NQ®

You get the behaviour that you reward. So what type of negotiating behaviour do you really want to see? Often there is a huge discrepancy between 'the walk' and 'the talk'. Remember that your reward system is an integral part of your negotiation infrastructure. It can play a key role, for example, in allowing you to formulate the extent to which a new trajectory must yield innovations, or how you value the strengthening of relations with customers or suppliers, or how you express appreciation towards your long-term partners. In fact, rewards can help you to control any aspect that has been defined as important to your business strategy.

It is also necessary to re-examine your basic business processes, such as promotion, with your new Corporate NQ® perspective in mind. Think about the age-old question of whether a leader can be both powerful and respected. Is it better to be loved or feared? Research has shown that cooperative managers are more beneficial for their organization, but achieve promotion less rapidly.[54] In other words, it is in the interests of the company to encourage negotiating managers, the NQ®-ers, by helping them to climb up the hierarchical ladder more quickly. But this is not always a simple matter. Our traditional stereotyped way of thinking means that tough managers often seem to be more capable – and they are certainly more openly ambitious. The best solution is to include 'negotiating' as a core competence for your management staff.

Reassessing these stereotypes will have implications for your incentive system, of which promotion is just one aspect (albeit an important one). For decades we have developed organizations with incentives (rewards *and* punishments) which were designed to encourage people to achieve public and commercial objectives. The theory was that if you wanted your staff to work hard, you had to pay them on the basis of their performance and results. In more recent years, however, the idea has been gaining ground that, in addition to carrots and sticks, it is also necessary to devise systems that are based on 'engagement, communication, a sense of common purpose and identity'. Many now believe that these systems can be just as effective as (or can at least supplement) their long-established forerunners.[55]

Spread the word!

Knowledge is power – an old adage that is equally applicable in the context of negotiations. However, by this we mean internal knowledge, since this is the type of knowledge that works to the benefit of the organization as a whole. Gathering a wide range of information about the trajectory of forthcoming negotiations, about your negotiating partners and about the subject of the discussions is a crucial element of the preparation process. So is sharing best practice, or avoiding knowledge leakage if people leave the company or move to another job in a different department.

It needs to be remembered that for many companies much of this still lies in the future. Corporate NQ® is still in its infancy. Only the most progressive 20% of companies have a formal negotiation debriefing process. Just 4% have begun with the creation of a formalized structure to ensure the dissemination of any knowledge gained during negotiations throughout the organization.[56]

A good practical example is Hewlett-Packard's 'Negotiator's Garage'. This is a dynamic, virtual environment (with tools) for negotiators. The elements available in this 'garage' include training, templates for the preparation of a negotiating strategy and a reference library of previous negotiations.[57]

In addition to the ubiquitous company database (which can usually be consulted via the intranet), there are numerous other innovative instruments for recording and internally transferring knowledge, experience and insights acquired in negotiations.

The Corporate NQ® negotiator

Here the circle is complete. The individual skills of the negotiators – in other words, the four keys – remain crucial throughout the entire process. It is still delicate, made-to-measure human work. But the individual objectives of a loose collection of one-off negotiations (insofar as these exist at all!) has now been brought into the framework of long-term objectives of the organization. Moreover, there is now a cooperative and supportive company mentality and infrastructure. In short, the (intelligent) negotiators now work within the context of Corporate NQ®.

Negotiating from an organizational perspective requires different skills and attitudes than those of the lone wolf. The lone wolf limits the number of people he allows to take part in the negotiating process, is first and foremost concerned with 'closing the deal', gives away as little information as possible, is competitive and attaches little importance to debriefing. In contrast, we know that an NQ®-er is cooperative, has a preference for win-win agreements and is transparent about his own interests.

The most important differences between a lone wolf and an organizational negotiator (a Corporate NQ®-er) are detailed in the following table.

	LONE WOLF	CORPORATE NQ®-ER
CHARACTER	› SOLOIST	› TEAM PLAYER
OBJECTIVE	› ALWAYS CLOSES A DEAL › CREATES SHORT-TERM VALUE › WIN-LOSE	› PURSUES ORGANIZATIONAL OBJECTIVES › CREATES LONG-TERM VALUE › WIN-WIN, LASTING RELATIONSHIPS
CONTEXT/TYPE OF ORGANIZATION	› SITUATIONAL/STACCATO/ITERATIVE › COMPETITIVE › LITTLE SUPERVISION	› INSTITUTIONAL/HOLISTIC › CHAIN PLAYER › LEARNING (TOGETHER)
INCENTIVES	› BONUS FOR RESULTS › FINANCE-ORIENTED	› BONUS FOR LONG-TERM VALUE DEALS FOR THE ORGANIZATION › BONUS FOR SATISFYING THE MOST IMPORTANT STAKEHOLDERS
SKILLS	› GIVES LITTLE INFORMATION › DOES NOT EVALUATE › DEFENDS OWN INTERESTS › SELDOM SHARES KNOWLEDGE	› IS COOPERATIVE/TRANSPARENT ABOUT INTERESTS › EVALUATES › IS ORGANIZATION-SENSITIVE › SHARES KNOWLEDGE
INSTRUMENTS	› OWN KNOWLEDGE AND EXPERIENCE	› OWN KNOWLEDGE AND EXPERIENCE + KNOWLEDGE MANAGEMENT

For the successful introduction and management of Corporate NQ®, it is essential that your most important negotiators are competent NQ®-ers. It is also recommended to appoint your best and most strategically well-placed NQ®-ers as your Corporate NQ® ambassadors. Make sure that there is a common negotiating language and a common negotiating paradigm throughout your organization. Gear your negotiation training to your specific negotiation strategy, processes and structure. In this way, your NQ®-ers and your Corporate NQ® will help to strengthen each other!

As an organisation with a high corporate NQ®, you know that...

... negotiation intelligence (NQ®) thrives best in an environment in which negotiation is regarded as a quality – an integral part of the organization as a whole. The ORGANIZATIONAL CONTEXT is a major factor in determining the success you can achieve with the four keys. Research has proven conclusively that it is possible to book substantial gains at this level. The journey towards Corporate NQ® is a fascinating, innovative, step-by-step process with high IMPACT.

As an organization, you take active steps to build this into your company's DNA. Just like NQ®, Corporate NQ® can be learned. This requires first of all the right Corporate NQ® mentality. An important element of this mentality is that negotiators should no longer think and act in situational terms, but in ORGANIZATIONAL TERMS: with a feeling for organizational sensitivity and an eye for both business strategy and BUSINESS DEVELOPMENT. This implies the need for STRUCTURES and INSTRUMENTS to support the NQ® negotiators in the course of their work. It is also important to adjust your system for incentives and REWARDS, so that the negotiators do not focus on short-term gains, but rather on securing strategic business objectives. And don't forget to facilitate KNOWLEDGE SHARING. Analyze what went well during the negotiations and what went less well. Then use this information to adjust your future planning.

Tips:

- Be aware of the existence of different negotiating contexts/frameworks and actively set about designing the one that best suits your organization.
- View negotiations as part of a long-term process of business development that goes far beyond the boundaries of individual negotiations.
- Develop, implement and maintain a negotiating infrastructure.
- Link your reward system for negotiation results to the achievement of strategic organizational objectives.
- Develop a knowledge policy based on best practice and lessons learnt from the negotiating process.
- As an organization, support value creation in the long term.

3

HANG YOUR KEYS ON THE RIGHT KEY-HOLDERS

'IT'S REALLY STRANGE: THE MORE I PRACTISE, THE MORE LUCK I SEEM TO HAVE.'

(Arnold Palmer, golfer)

So far, we have discussed the four keys that can unlock the door to successful negotiations. But you need to be able to put your keys somewhere, to hang them on the right hooks or key-holders. If you fail to do this, you risk losing your keys or not being able to find them when you really need to use them. While key-holders cannot unlock doors, they are just as essential as the keys themselves. To prove the point, consider the case of the following negotiator who hung her keys on the wrong hooks.

Mandy Ayers is the director of a highly successful logistics company. Mindy-Logistics has grown large, thanks to a combination of quality, hard work and punctual delivery. In recent years, the company has invested heavily in new technology. As a result, they are now market leaders in temperature-controlled transport.

The company was founded in a small provincial town by Mandy's father Benny Ayers. In the beginning, it was just small player in the market, struggling to survive against the competition from larger, well-established companies. At this time, the undisputed market leader was Mega-Logistics, a major player from a neighbouring city. The company chairman, John Boulder, was also the head of the employer's federation for the sector. He was an influential man, fully at home in the better social and political circles. He could perhaps best be described as an industrial potentate. When Mandy (still studying economics at the time) accompanied her father to the sector's New Year reception, Boulder could hardly conceal his contempt. After a glass or two too many, he drunkenly announced in a loud voice that the "peasants from the provinces" were lacking in culture and that to manage a major company you needed to "think big" – something that was beyond "the hicks from the sticks". It was clear he meant

Benny and his daughter. Every moment of that meeting with 'the devil' has remained engraved in Mandy's mind ever since.

But times change and so do economic circumstances. Pride, as they say, comes before a fall. Mega-Logistics realized far too late that it should have modernized its fleet with new technology. The typical Mega-Logistics customers were builders who could not care less about temperature fluctuations. The company was lulled into a false sense of security by the reasonably constant demand for bulk transport while the more lucrative markets were developing around tailor-made logistics and integration in ever more complex supply chains. In short, Mega-Logistics was lulled into a false sense of security by companies that required the delivery of large batches, whereas the profitable end of the market was switching towards more made-to-measure deliveries and increasingly complex supply chains.

The location in a major city suddenly became a handicap: there was no room for expansion and a lack of competent staff, since all the best people were snapped up by the city's many multinational companies which offered much greater financial rewards. And while Mega-Logistics gradually fell into decline, Mindy-Logistics slowly moved into a position of prominence. Thanks to a strategy of 'customer intimacy', it developed into an ever-stronger link in the logistical chain, with a seemingly limitless supply of qualified personnel and with the full support of the local community for its ambitious expansion plans.

In the meantime, John Boulder Jr. had taken over the running of the family business from his father. He was a slim, attractive, aristocratic figure, who made a good impression everywhere he went – except with his customers, who found him distant, reserved and calculating. The building sector was used to an informal way of doing business: a strong handshake and the ability to sink half a dozen beers in quick time were more important than a diploma in law and an MBA from the country's most prestigious business school.

Then the day arrived when Mindy-Logistics became bigger than Mega-Logistics at last. The city-slickers even lost their biggest customer to the provincial peasants. Mandy and her father cracked open a bottle of champagne that evening. The tide had turned completely.

Two years later John Boulder Jr. phoned Mandy on the phone. He wanted to sell his company. Mandy could hardly keep the tears from her eyes. Sadly, her father had died six months earlier – she would have loved to share this news with him. But she would take revenge in his place. She would buy up Boulder's company and would humiliate them in the process. She already looked forward to the day when the 'Mega-Logistics' name would be removed from their production hall alongside the motorway, to be replaced by a brand-new Mindy-Logistics logo.

But six months later Mandy looked back on the deal with dissatisfaction. Her financial director reluctantly confessed to her that many people in the sector were whispering that she had paid 50% too much for her 'prize'. The layout of the central depot on the edge of the city is hopelessly outdated and almost impossible to adjust to the needs of modern, integrated logistics. The trucks are log-jammed for hours on end and one-third of the old Mega-Logistics customers are a viable commercial proposition.

Mandy lies awake at night. Her dream has turned into a nightmare. At least she has succeeded in one thing: there is no Boulder working in the company any longer. The culminating act of humiliation came when she forced the now near-senile John Boulders Sr. to sign the final deed of transfer in the warehouse where Mindy-Logistics had first begun. For the occasion, she had specially mounted a huge photograph of her father. How proud he would have been!

The mistakes that Mandy made are recognizable and understandable. When we negotiate, we often let our sensitivities get the better of us. Our irrational side, our history, our dreams and our fears all come rushing to the surface, whether we want them to or not. In this sense, the behaviour of a negotiator is a complete package. Put another way: it is conditioned by both conscious and unconscious elements. These elements can be wise and foolish. They can be well-considered and impulsive. Seen from a purely rational perspective, we continually make 'mistakes' in our negotiations. We often leave too much added value lying unused on the table.

Economists tell us boldly that we seldom or never obtain the optimum deal. But this is hardly surprising. Negotiations are a highly complex interpersonal activity. As a result, everything 'human' – with all that this implies – has its place at the negotiating table. Consequently, we use negotiations to settle old scores, to massage our own egos, to achieve our cherished ideals, etc. Sometimes we are acutely aware of these less rational aspects. On other occasions we are hardly aware of them at all.

Usually, we make a sharp distinction between our 'smart' conscious mind and our 'stupid' unconscious mind. After all, we are capable of deliberately planning, focusing, and reasoning. Everyone knows that we have millions and millions of little grey cells, where we can store our long-term plans, make logical analyses of problems and split up our final objectives into more easily manageable intermediary targets. But we can also be subject to differing moods and emotions. Fear, anger and depression can all take over our thinking. This usually leads us to put forward 'stupid' arguments. As a result, the above distinction is too radical. Our conscious mind can be both intelligent and idiotic. Just listen to the 'reasoned' arguments of the smoker, even though he knows beyond doubt that cigarettes are bad for his health. His arguments hold no water – as is often the case with people who are convinced of the 'rightness' of their own cause. The counterarguments of others are simply brushed aside, almost without consideration.

How is this possible? How many essentially stupid, yet perfectly conscious arguments have you been forced to listen to in circumstances of this kind? You have probably lost count. On the reverse side of the coin, our unconscious mind is the product of millions of years of evolution. If you hear a loud bang, you will instinctively duck. You protect your body from perceived danger. This is a 'smart' function. In other words, our unconscious can also be extremely clever.

As a result of these various permutations, there are four typical human mental processes involved in negotiating situations. These are the workings of the smart conscious mind, the stupid conscious mind, the smart unconscious mind and the stupid unconscious mind.

THE SMART CONSCIOUS MIND

Negotiators all think that they are clever and in distributive negotiations they probably think that they are sly as well. They dream up all different kinds of strategy, they analyze the situation, they identify their BATNA and ZOPA, they weigh up pros and cons. In the smart conscious mind, negotiations are a game of chess, where every move is well considered in advance and has a specific purpose. All we need to do is keep a cool head – and success will be ours! In a sense, most negotiators want to be 'more clever' that their negotiating partners. Fair enough, but this is not as simple as it sounds. If you nevertheless hope to achieve this ideal, you need a key-holder with three big hooks.

Hook 1: Always keep your eyes focused on the final objective

Test everything that happens – absolutely everything – against your final objective. Insults, setbacks, successes: examine them all calmly and assess to what extent they help you to reach your ultimate goal. Remember the famous lines from Rudyard Kipling's poem 'If', which is written on the wall of the players' entrance to the Centre Court at Wimbledon: 'If you can meet with triumph and disaster, and treat those two impostors just the same...' Keeping a cool head means checking every development in the negotiation against your final objective – in a calm, careful and considered manner.

Hook 2: Request and register more information

We have already mentioned that the best negotiators are curious by nature. Your smart conscious mind needs more information to function effectively than its stupid counterpart. The stupid conscious mind has a tendency to fixate on a single (and usually emotional) factor. This is why it is so difficult to remain 'smartly aware' when we are talking about ourselves, our jobs, our family. Our conscious mind finds it hard to deal with these subjects rationally. The only way to counter this is to keep on asking questions, giving answers, passing and receiving information. The more data you have, the more likely you are to remain rational. Consult more second opinions and keep exploring alternative lines of thought.

Hook 3: Combine the information at your disposal in a logical and coherent manner

Make a model that clearly shows how each intermediate step brings you closer to your final objective. Split the data into smaller blocks and then reassemble these blocks in different ways. Compile a list of advantages and disadvantages. Finally, draw a clear diagram that brings all these different elements together and shows how they relate to each other and to your ultimate goal.

THE STUPID CONSCIOUS MIND

No matter how hard we try, there are some things for which our conscious mind is simply not smart enough. When discussing Key 2 we warned against the danger of short cuts. Unfortunately, this tendency to take short-cuts is deeply rooted in our human nature. Whether we like it or not, for some keys there are simply no practical hooks on our key hanger. If your partner reads out a list of twenty random numbers, you will (probably) not be able to repeat them all. We accept this kind of mental challenge as being beyond the powers of our memory. But for other challenges we are less willing to accept that our 'lazy' brains have let us down again. Just 'trying harder' is not enough; it doesn't help. Fortunately, our brains have the ability to be consciously smart – very smart, in fact. But always trying to be consciously smart is very tiring. For this reason our brain makes use of all kinds of mental short cuts. In other words, it likes to keep things simple. And in daily life these short cuts usually work. But in a complex environment (and most negotiations are very complex), our smart conscious mind can often do very stupid things. Consider the following example. If you want to drive away with your car, you need to depress the gas pedal. Therefore, driving away = giving the car gas. And driving away quickly = giving it plenty of gas. This is a simple rule, often referred to as a heuristic. But this is where things can start to get tricky. Imagine that your car is bogged down in the mud. Your simple rule no longer applies. Giving it gas will only sink you deeper into the mud. Instead, you need to get out of the car (which implies a loss of time), find a plank, put it under your wheel, and accelerate slowly. If the situation is complex, your short cut won't work.

Two colleagues are working on the same complex investment portfolio. However, they have ignored their planning. As a result, their deadline is approaching more rapidly than they expected, so that they start to put each other under pressure. 'Didn't we agree that...?' While referring to previously made agreements is usually a relevant approach in work situations, doing so immediately prior to an important deadline may cause unnecessary irritation.

Situations where the 'normal' working methods of our smart conscious mind are no longer effective are known as cognitive biases. Even a well-trained and highly-motivated conscious mind can find it difficult to avoid these mental traps. Dozens of research projects have shown that our brains go 'off the track' in certain circumstances and take decisions that are far from optimal.[58] However hard we try to 'think', we still keep making mistakes.

Moreover, our stupid unconscious mind, driven by moods and emotions, has an even stronger tendency to strengthen these cognitive biases. Have you ever listened to the intellectual quality of the arguments put forward in a messy divorce case? They have very little to do with logic or reason. Similarly, Mandy Ayers was misled by her cognitive bias into underestimating her opponent, an error that was further intensified by her desire for revenge.

During negotiations cognitive biases are an important factor in two key elements: how we make 'mistakes' and how we assess the way in which the other side is likely to make mistakes. This is what makes negotiation such a fascinating and often addictive 'game'. If we make decisions alone, we have to rely exclusively on our own judgement to avoid cognitive biases. If we make decisions with the other party in a pure problem-solving context, the other party will help to stimulate our lazy brain. Herein lies the great difference between the 'stupid' win-lose approach to negotiations and the 'smart' win-win strategy.

If you see negotiations as a game that you must win, then you can only hope that your opponent will be misled once or twice by his cognitive biases. You can even 'help' him trip, for example with time pressure or alcohol – two tried and tested methods of triggering the cognitive biases.

However, if you regard negotiations as a win-win exercise, you will actually warn the other party when they are in danger of falling prey to their own cognitive biases, allowing them to reorder their thoughts and data in such a manner that the effect of the bias can be kept to a minimum. Tricks involving time and alcohol will become unnecessary, since you are no longer engaged in a contest but in a collaborative venture.

Here are some of the most common cognitive biases in negotiating situations.

Dangerous hook 1: Random anchor points

We have already mentioned the importance of 'smart anchoring' in connection with Key 1 and Key 3. Anchors are hugely important in negotiations. But anchors also work even if they are not relevant. Random anchors, cast by chance or without thought, can also affect our way of thinking.

Imagine that you are negotiating the price of a piece of pre-Columbian art. The current market value is around 10,000 euros. But just before the serious haggling starts, a professor of art history examines the work and mumbles in your ear: "These things change hands for 50,000 euros nowadays". "Are you an expert, Professor?" you ask in amazement. "No, not really," he replies. "My speciality is the Italian Renaissance." Unwittingly, the professor has cast a random anchor. In reality, he doesn't really know what he is talking about. Even so, you will still start to doubt the opening offer of 7,000 euros that you previously had in mind. The 50,000 euros are locked into your brain. The interfering academic has 'anchored' you in a much higher price range. And experts are not the only source of this. Pseudo-experts, newspaper articles, television reports: they all continually throw out anchor points left, right and centre. And even though they are random, we still allow ourselves to be influenced by them. We just can't help ourselves.

Dangerous hook 2: Assessing loss differently from gain

Not winning ten euros is something most of us prefer to losing ten euros. If you find ten euros in the street but then lose it again, you will feel irritated, even though you are no worse off than before. Similarly, we only truly value our honour, our health and our friends once we have lost them. This is a very 'human' reaction, but it is not really logical. It is just that we hate loss. And our hatred of losing is stronger than our love of winning. This insight is a hook that every negotiator must be able to recognize – and turn to his advantage. We have already seen that the intelligent negotiator uses Key 1 to actually limit the loss of the other side. For example, he does his very best to ensure that his negotiating partner does not suffer any loss of face. In our discussion of Key 4, we also stressed the importance of framing. Many experts still regard the win-loss strategy as the strongest negotiating framework. People hate loss more than they fear uncertainty. Above all, it is their uncertainty about potential loss that makes them nervous. For this reason, it is important that a win-win negotiator should always underline what the other side will lose, if you fail to reach a mutually acceptable agreement. It is equally important to emphasize what has already been achieved – since this, too, will be lost if no final agreement is possible. In the case study involving Mandy, it is clear that she became the victim of her own desire for revenge. She has never been able to forget the sense of loss that she felt as a result of her humiliation at the hands of the Boulders when she was young. Blinded by this emotional perception, she fails to realize that she, too, has probably humiliated people in her time and also forgets all the words of praise and genuine appreciation that other colleagues have lavished on her in recent years. Nor can she imagine or appreciate that the hated Boulders actually admire her now and in fact are even jealous of her! Her assessment of loss gives her a distorted view of the real picture – and so she makes the wrong decision about the price.

Dangerous hook 3: Having a false impression of the negotiating situation

It is never wise to confuse your own wishes with reality. But it is equally pointless to assume that your fears reflect reality. Even so, this is a mistake that many negotiators continue to make. They form an impression of the negotiating situation in their own mind that is often far removed from the truth. Here are a number of common scenarios:

> Negotiators have a tendency to undervalue any proposal made by the other side, simply because it comes from the other side and must therefore be 'suspect'. (This is known in the jargon as reactive devaluation.) Likewise, they tend to overvalue their own proposals, simply because they are the product of their own brilliant mind!

> Negotiators often think that their only option is to divide up the cake. They forget that it is also possible to try and increase the size of that cake. As we discussed at length with reference to Key 1 and Key 2, most of us will have been confronted with this at one point in time or another.

> Negotiators always opt for escalation, even if an objective analysis shows that it might be wiser simply to change your strategy.

> Negotiators often think that the other side has the same preferences as they do and therefore will present irreconcilable proposals.

The dozens of cognitive biases to which people are subject can be conveniently condensed into a single basic principle: everything that can help you to convince or influence the opposing party, everything that can help you to 'prove your right' will seldom be of benefit to your own decision-making process and will seldom help you to actually 'secure your right'. 'Securing your right' is based on analysis, a methodical approach, discussable proposals and nuanced evaluations. 'Proving your right' relies on striking examples, fantastic anecdotes, emotional appeals and memorable stories. This is something that every teacher, every salesmen and every preacher will tell you. But those same astounding stories, those same exaggerated examples and those same thrilling emotions are generally a barrier to clear thinking. So always be on your guard against out-of-the ordinary, emotional and 'unique' proposals. Our brains reason on the basis of analogy – they are seldom purely analytical. If a situation reminds us of some other successful situation in the past, this is often enough to persuade us to take the plunge with exaggerated self-confidence. This is the basis of the so-called 'saliency bias': if something is too salient or too eye-catching, it is nearly always dangerous for your reasoning and decision-making.

THE SMART UNCONSCIOUS MIND

Many negotiators will tell you that they negotiate first and foremost on the basis of their 'gut feeling'. They can 'sense' what is happening and know intuitively when to act. The timing and nature of their proposals, their decisions to accept or reject counter-offers – these are all things that they do more or less unconsciously, as though they are operating on automatic pilot. You hear this kind of comment most frequently from highly experienced negotiators, which suggests that our claim for the existence of a smart unconscious mind is not as silly as it might first sound. And we are not alone. Experts in the field of intuitive decision-making are now in general agreement that expertise of any kind is almost unthinkable without 'intelligent intuition' and that such intuition can only be developed after long, direct and very varied experience.[59] Anyone whose negotiations have been confined to a single culture can hardly be expected to have any intuitive feeling for intercultural differences. Anyone who limits their negotiating strategy to an uncompromising win-lose approach will have little intuitive idea of when and how to make the switch from 'hard' to 'soft'.

A word of warning, however. In most cases, 'gut feeling' will actually turn out to be another form of cognitive bias. You can only negotiate this way in very specific circumstances and on the basis of extensive, varied and relevant experience. All too often, gut feeling is just another way to describe prejudice, unsupported assumptions and even mindless superstition.

The role of intuition in negotiations is still unexplored territory. Very few scientific studies have been carried out in this area. For this reason, our comments on 'intelligent intuition' are based largely on analogies drawn from other fields of inquiry.

First and foremost, intuition is a warning signal. It tells you that there is danger ahead. For this reason, it makes sense that (experienced!) negotiators should reject a proposal if it somehow 'doesn't seem right'. However, the reverse is not true: the fact that your intuition tells you that 'this is a great deal' is no guarantee. It is always best to check and analyse the facts and figures once more before you commit yourself.

Intuition is more useful (and reliable) when dealing with people, rather than with facts and figures. If you sense that a person is not quite what he seems, you should double your guard. If you sense that a figure is not quite what it seems, this doesn't really get you anywhere. There are dozens of studies that prove conclusively that our intuition with regard to logic, numbers and statistics is only poorly developed. You can look at it this way: our intuition with regard to people is based on our own experience since birth, supplemented by the lessons of our education and upbringing. This is a very rich and varied source of experience. In contrast, our direct experience (for example) of the facts and figures relating to global warming is minimal by comparison. How many periods of major climate change have you actually lived through?

Experts who take reliable intuitive decisions simply seem to have received more signals than the rest of us. Negotiating experts who try to give you 'rules to sharpen your intuition' (for example, watch where the other person sits at the negotiating table, are their shoes polished, are they sweating, is their use of language rational and reasonable, etc.) are nothing more than pseudo-experts. This does not mean that you should not be aware of all these points and their possible significance, but a real intuitive expert can sense and combine all these things almost symbiotically. His strength lies in his ability to interpret and amalgamate different signals, rather than relying on a single powerful signal.

The most trustworthy intuitions seem to be 'first impressions'. When judging others, 'thin slices' are usually enough to allow us to form a reliable opinion. Research has confirmed this in a series of spectacular studies, which show that after as little as thirty seconds our intuitive assessment of a person is consistently more accurate than a wild guess. And this applies equally to salesmen and university lecturers! But does it also apply in a negotiating situation? Two researchers at the renowned Massachusetts Institute of Technology have looked into this matter.[60] Jared Curland and Alex Pentland examined whether the conversation dynamics of the first five minutes of the negotiations were a reliable indicator of the final outcome. 112 MBA students conducted a simulated negotiation between an employer (a vice-president) and an employee (a manager). During the first five minutes of each conversation the researchers measured 'thin slice' behaviour. How much time did the negotiator spend speaking? How forcefully did the negotiator take control of the discussions? With how much emphasis did the negotiator speak? How intensively did the negotiator mirror the behaviour of the other person? The measurements were extremely sophisticated and the parameters were set using a highly complex computer analysis. On the basis of these parameters, it was predicted how successful the negotiator would be in terms of his own perspective. The predictive reliability of the 'thin slice' behaviour was even stronger than in other comparable studies. Your body language betrays what is likely to happen from the very first minutes of meeting someone. But not every type of behaviour was relevant in every situation. For predicting things from the perspective of a boss, the amount of time he spent speaking was most relevant. For the employees, it was the extent to which they were able to mirror the boss' behaviour. If you talk with emphasis and accentuate your words, the prospects for a successful outcome are not good: you will later score less well than your adversary and he will score correspondingly better. Apparently, too much emphasis is a sign of insecurity and betrays a feeling of dependence on the other person – signals which this other person is very quick to pick up.

THE STUPID UNCONSCIOUS MIND

Negotiators are people. And people have weaknesses. These weakness are often described as 'sins', 'desires', 'failings' or even 'human foibles'. In an economic context, the concept of 'animal spirits' is most commonly used, whereas the Christian tradition speaks of the 'seven deadly sins'. These 'passions' and 'moods' are easily recognizable, but surprisingly enough they have seldom been systematically studied in relation to negotiations, with the exception of the worst (according to 'The Divine Comedy') of the deadly sins: pride. In modern terms, we would probably describe this as 'excessive self-confidence'. Nearly all negotiators suffer from this defect. They believe that the negotiation will inevitably turn out in their favour. And because both sides think exactly the same, it is easy to understand how negotiators often mistake their wishes for reality. If there are one hundred units to be divided at the negotiating table and if both parties are convinced that 65 of these units will be theirs, it is clearly possible to speak of systematic bias.

Mandy allowed herself to get carried away by her stupid unconscious mind. She thought that she was unbeatable, that she would show the world just how good she really was. It simply wasn't possible for those arrogant idiots from Mega-Logistics to get the better of her at the negotiating table. Had she not shown in recent years that she knew how to run a business while they didn't? This is the core of excessive self-confidence. Rather like when you are buying stocks and shares, past performance is no guarantee of future performance. Mandy had certainly had successes in recent times, but she had no experience whatsoever of negotiating with someone who had humiliated her so badly in the past – with someone whose company had always been much bigger and stronger than hers, with someone who had only been interested in money and not in the needs of the sector. And here we can see how the stupid unconscious mind is 'helped' by its stupid conscious counterpart. Mandy thought – wrongly – that the other party was just like her.

With a good understanding of the right key hooks for your higher NQ®, you know that...

... negotiation is a typically HUMAN activity. Even if we possess the four basic keys of negotiating intelligence, we can still sometimes fail to find them when we need them, because we have hung them on the wrong hooks of our key holder. The negotiator is subject to all human weaknesses – just like the rest of us. His SMART CONSCIOUS MIND helps him to stay calm, to focus continually on his final objective, to maintain the coherence of the big picture and, above all, to consult as many sources and register as much information as possible. But that same conscious mind can sometimes be extremely stupid as well. Some key hooks seem very attractive, but if we put our keys there we may never find them again – or, at least, not in time to be of any use. These COGNITIVE BIASES are the red hooks of danger, deceptive mental forks in the road that can easily mislead us and take us down the wrong path. They include random anchor points, fear of the possibility of loss and a wrong view of the negotiating situation. In fact, the reader should see this book as a permanent invitation to constantly amend his view of negotiations. Negotiators also have an unconscious mind. This, too, can sometimes behave stupidly. If we allow ourselves to be the plaything of our unconscious moods and passions, we can never make best use of our negotiating intelligence. In short, we will have been hijacked by our unconscious demons. Fortunately, our unconscious mind can also be smart. INTELLIGENT INTUITION is an important component of negotiating intelligence. Sensing what is going to happen and feeling whether you can trust the other person are both important hooks for your negotiating keys.

The following tips will help you to guard against cognitive biases, so that you can choose the right key hooks to hang your NQ® keys onto:

- Never make decisions on the basis of a single bizarre argument, no matter how attractive or convincing it might seem.
- If it *seems* too good to be true, then it probably *is* too good to be true.
- You can trust your intuition, if it warns you about the behavioural patterns of the other person. We have a radar for other people.
- Don't accept an agreement if your intuition tells you it doesn't feel right. Sleep on it, ask for a second opinion and check again the arguments for and against.
- Watch out for EXCESSIVE SELF-CONFIDENCE. Past success is no guarantee for future success.
- Be aware that few negotiators are able to keep their head cool when faced with the prospect of loss.

4

IF YOUR KEYS FALL INTO THE WRONG HANDS: AT THE NEGOTIATING TABLE WITH MACHIAVELLI

'I TRUST MOST OF THE PEOPLE I PLAY CARDS WITH – BUT I PREFER TO DEAL THE CARDS MYSELF.'

(after John O'Loughlin)

Ben & Jerry's's are well known for their excellent ice cream, their alternative way of doing business and their high ethical standards. The company name is a combination of the first names of the two founders, Ben Cohen and Jerry Greenfield. These two friends were the 'losers' in their class. At a complete loss, they decided that there was not much point in studying and so they agreed to set up a business instead. After careful consideration, they concluded that the only thing they knew anything about was food. They wanted to start with bagels, but they didn't have enough money to buy a bagel machine. And so they hit on the idea of selling ice cream. They took a ten-dollar written course on ice cream making and opened a shop in Vermont. It was a spectacular success. Their ice cream was tasty, creamy and contained a good portion of nuts, a huge splattering of chocolate and plenty of exotic fruits that most Americans had never heard of. There was also a great atmosphere in the shop. Ben and Jerry were anarchist hippies, with a house musician playing jazz!

They had no business plan, no marketing plan, no financial plan. In fact, they had no plans at all. But this wasn't a problem... until the winter came. Winters in Vermont tend to be long and cold. Not exactly the ideal weather for an ice cream parlour. And so Cohen and Greenfield – out of necessity – began delivering to restaurants and supermarkets. Unfortunately, they didn't have the required logistical infrastructure so they turned for help to the distributors of the absolute market leader in the ice cream sector: Häagen-Dazs. At first, this worked – but after a time the people at H-D began to look at things more closely. Why should these hippies from Vermont get 'free rides' for their products at the company's expense? The negotiations between Häagen-Dazs, the transporters and Ben & Jerry's were extremely short. Häagen-Dazs gave the transporters a simple choice: they either shipped the huge quantities of Häagen-Dazs or the comparatively miniscule quantities of Ben & Jerry's. They were free to choose. But, of course there was no choice, really. Häagen-Dazs had simply used its power to force through a deal that was exclusively in its own favour. It was a question of 'take it or leave it'.

Ben & Jerry's didn't take this lying down. On the contrary, they went on the counter-attack. They looked for the weak spot in the Häagen-Dazs armour and found it in the shape of the mother company, Pillsbury. At that time the Pillsbury group not only included Häagen-Dazs, but also companies such as Burger King and Green Giant. The symbol of the Pillsbury group was the Pillsbury doughboy, a funny little doll-like figure with a fat belly. Ben & Jerry's launched a campaign with stickers, fun videos and one-man picket-lines in front of the Pillsbury HQ, all asking the same question: 'What is the doughboy afraid of?' The press were soon enjoying this battle of David against Goliath, and took up the theme enthusiastically. Even the grandson of the chairman of the Pillsbury board begged granddad to leave Ben & Jerry's's alone! Häagen-Dazs had the legal and economic arguments on their side, and in theory it was a battle they should never have lost. They were 'right', but they were unable to convince others that they were right. Under the pressure of public opinion, they agreed that one of their potentially largest rivals could continue to make use of their distribution channels, channels that they had built up at great time and expense. The Trojan horse had been taken inside![61]

WHY BE ON THE LOOK-OUT FOR DIRTY TRICKS?

If you read a standard manual on coaching or conversation techniques, you will seldom see a section called 'Dirty Tricks' or 'Machiavellian Moves'. It is very different with negotiation. No book is complete without an extensive chapter on the dark arts of lying, cheating and manipulation. The reason for this is fairly obvious. As we have mentioned earlier in this book, negotiation is an attempt to find a dynamic balance between interests that are 'his', 'mine' and 'ours'. We hope that we have made clear that intelligent negotiation means constantly pursuing win-win, by seeking to enlarge the ZOPA and showing proper respect for the concerns of the other side. But not everyone sees negotiation as win-win. Both Häagen-Dazs and Ben & Jerry's's were only interested in their own share of the market. And they both knew that this could only be increased at the expense of the other. Rightly or wrongly, this means that we sometimes get the impression that our negotiating partner is only concerned with his own best interests. Or worse still, we sometimes think that he is of 'bad faith' or even wants to do us harm. We think that we are negotiating with the devil![62]

In this sense, negotiations often have an uncomfortable and irritating undertone. You need to be constantly on your guard. *Caveat emptor,* as the Romans said 'buyer beware'. Apparently already our Latin forefathers were well aware that people in business are more than capable of cheating – especially the seller. Not much has changed in the 21st century. Negotiators can be just as devious and dishonest. Aggressive, unethical and deliberately misleading tactics still suit some modern negotiating styles. However, they are wholly inappropriate for certain other styles. Academic research has shown that competitively minded negotiators are still prepared to play fast and loose with the truth. But this is not our way. If we argue in this book for win-win negotiations and a high level of NQ®, then hopefully it should be self-evident that we do not intend to provide you with a whole list of dirty tricks that you can employ.

Having said that, the basic position of our book is equally clear: be friendly, open and cooperative... but not naïve! There are still plenty of lone wolves out there, who are just waiting to get their teeth into some nice, gullible lambs. There is an old story which says that if you go into a room full of people and you know in advance that one of them is an idiot but you don't know which one, chances are that it is you. It is better to anticipate the use of dirty tricks and plan your reaction. Otherwise, you may only discover them when it is already too late.

What is manipulation?

Manipulation is a tactic than can only work when the other person does not realize what is going on. If my boss promises me a juicy bonus if I can meet a tight deadline, that is not manipulation. Next time I will probably work even harder if there is the prospect of another fat reward. But consider the following scenario. A CEO has four different managers working in four different locations. He tells each of them the same thing: 'You are my best man, the only one I can really trust.' He then gossips about the other three, suggesting that they are incompetent and cannot be relied on. This massages the ego of the so-called 'better' manager, so that he works harder. This *is* manipulation – but it will only work until the four managers get together around the same table.

BLACK, GREY AND WHITE DIRTY TRICKS

Black tricks

Dirty tricks in negotiations are manipulative methods that: (1) deliberately damage the other party; and (2) no longer work once the other person catches on. The very dirtiest of these tricks also have a very clear negative moral connotation. For this reason, we call them black tricks. They have much in common with the way that the illegal trafficking of arms brings great financial rewards to the gun-runners or rape bring sexual pleasure to the ruthless offender. In business, blackmail is a good example. While these tricks work, their mechanisms are offensive and often even repulsive. For most observers of negotiations, these black tricks fall into two main categories: barefaced lying and destabilization.

Lying during negotiations is not only unethical (but see further!), it is also very risky. If your lies are uncovered, you put yourself in a very weak position. You can instantly forget about any kind of win-win deal. The other side will have lost its trust and will be out to get you!

If you decide to take the risk anyway, the 'most powerful' lies are often those related to the BATNA. We discussed this in respect of Key 3: a negotiator is only as strong as his best alternative. Even so, negotiators are sometimes prepared to lie about their BATNA. Occasionally, they even create non-existent or 'ghost' BATNAS: another party that is ready to sign, will pay cash, is pushing hard for a deal, or something similar.

Trying to emotionally destabilize the other person is perhaps the most despicable tactic of all, yet there are still negotiators who are proud of themselves once they have successfully achieved it. The most classic method is to keep your negotiating partner waiting much longer than is necessary. Nobody likes waiting and most of us get nervous if we are forced to wait. But this nervousness is nothing in comparison with effects of the cruellest (almost criminal) destabilization methods. We are all susceptible to destabilization by sex and drugs and rock-'n-roll. If you can present it as your norm to have a stiff glass or two before a meeting and if you can ensure that your opposite negotiating party is not prepared for this, the results are not difficult to imagine. If you can then collect a number of incriminating photographs, you can rest assured that your negotiating 'partner' will be thoroughly destabilized. Most people would regard such practice as disgusting and morally unacceptable. Fortunately, the genuinely criminal forms of destabilization, such as bribery, remain confined to a very limited number of sectors and situations.

Grey tricks

Negotiations – and negotiating tricks – are seldom a black-and-white affair. Between black and white there are numerous shades of grey tricks, which are often seen as 'normal' and are even regarded by some negotiators as morally defensible – or at least as not being openly 'immoral'. Whether or not they are ethically responsible is another matter – and a matter that raises much furious debate. The list of these grey tricks is almost endless. Here is a brief summary of some of the more common ones:

- "My hands are tied: I would like to help, but the decision doesn't rest with me."
- "I am bound by the requirements of a higher good." (A vague code of ethics, a company rule, etc.).
- Exhaustion: making the other person negotiate alone, while you use several different negotiators.
- Intimidating locations: prestigious surroundings, expensive hotels, historical buildings.
- Exotic locations, calculated to create strange sensations – and therefore confusion – in the other person.
- Physical intimidation: allowing no time for recovery from jet-lag, use of temperature variations, offering too much or too little food and drink, etc.
- Good cop/bad cop: the 'nice' negotiator seems reasonable in comparison with the 'nasty' negotiator.
- Demanding advantageous general conditions on the basis of a single exceptional case (a handicapped employee, a life-saving delivery, etc.).
- Demanding a final last-minute concession immediately before the signing of the deal. In shipping circles, for example, the Greek companies are notorious for demanding a free anchor once they have agreed to buy a new ship.
- Raising irrelevant issues: adding meaningless (but seemingly important) demands to a really crucial demand, and then generously 'conceding' these first two minor points, so that the big fish can be landed.

These grey tricks are often compared with the behaviour of poker players. Like dishonest negotiators, they bluff, they spin you a line and they distract you with ambiguous comments, so that you no longer know what's real and what isn't. But they draw the line at fixing the deal or installing mirrors to read your hand. Chicanery of the latter kind is reserved exclusively for the users of black tricks!

White tricks

White dirty tricks? It almost sounds like a contradictio in terminis. White tricks are the tricks that are generally accepted by everyone. They often continue to work, even when everyone knows exactly what is going on. If your daughter tells you: 'You're the best mummy in the whole wide world!' but immediately follows this with a request for a piece of chocolate, you know precisely what she is playing at – but she still walks off with the chocolate. Flattery works!

This is the problem with white tricks: it is not really clear whether they are morally reprehensible or not. As we have just seen, they are often very transparent. And we know that the other party is using them to secure his own advantage. Yet we fall for them time and again. In one sense, we are 'tricking' ourselves and we regard the outcome as ethically acceptable in normal circumstances between grown adults. If we listen too attentively to all that flattery, if we accept all those carelessly thrown anchor points, if we allow ourselves to believe in the mock dismay of our negotiating partners, there are few people who would say that we are being morally abused!

The white zone is often created – or almost creates itself – through actions that are all-too-human, so that to some extent we all have a degree of affinity with the resulting tricks. Many of them are variations on the following themes:

- Encourage the other party's self-overestimation. Flatter him, charm him, say how much you can learn from him, allow him a small victory here, stroke his ego there...and then move in for the kill. Once he is blinded by his own ego, he will start to neglect details, so that he will eventually fall into the trap that he has partially dug for himself. Every manipulator knows that flattery helps, so lay it on thick. You don't catch flies with vinegar. Sugar is the business!

- Create intellectual confusion in the other person's mind. Make the negotiations more complex than is necessary. The other person will not want to admit that he doesn't understand the complexities (ego again!) and so will be more ready to make concessions. In short, he won't see the wood for the trees!
- Set a few 'dangerous' anchor points. You can let these drop casually or, better still, get someone else to drop them for you: the results of other negotiations, the outcome of new research, the opinions of experts. All these anchors 'coincidentally' seem to work in your favour. But that's not your fault, is it?

THE TWILIGHT ZONE BETWEEN GREY AND BLACK: SOMETHING FOR THE ETHICISTS

If only it was all straightforward and easy! Unfortunately, there is a large twilight zone between the really black dirty tricks and the lighter grey tricks that somehow don't seem so bad. Of course, all these tricks – grey or black – would be rejected out of hand in normal everyday circumstances, but in a world where negotiation is often seen as a battle, the moral imperatives are not so clear-cut. For some negotiators it really is a question of 'all's fair in love and war!' This grey-black area is the playground of the ethicists. For example, some target groups (as we shall see shortly) still find it ethically acceptable to lie during negotiations – an attitude that is clearly open to discussion. We have already mentioned on more than one occasion that the basic rules of the negotiating game have a significant impact on the likely negotiation results. And by now it should be evident that the large majority of negotiators still regard the game as a competitive one in which the use of bluff, the withholding of information and the misrepresentation of interests are all 'legitimate' tactics. The level of ethical responsibility drops even further if the negotiations are seen as a one-off event – an anonymous transaction with no future perspective. By contrast, it is the so-called 'shadow of the future' that really seems to make negotiators stick within ethical boundaries.

Roy Lewicki, himself a very charming and morally correct person, has systematically investigated the tactics used by negotiators in this grey-black zone.[63] He identified eighteen different types of problem behaviour. With the help of statistical analysis, he reduced these types to just five major elements, which summarize with considerable accuracy the tricks most frequently used at the negotiating table. He even developed a scale on which to grade them: the SINS scale. The resulting five most fundamental tactics (sins) of negotiators are as follows:

> Fighting tooth and nail for your own interests, with no concern for anyone or anything else. This includes tactics such as concealing your BATNA or making an extremely high opening bid. These are recommendations that you often find in the popular literature or in seminars about 'negotiating for winners'.

> Attacking the other person's network. This includes talking directly to their key contacts, such as bosses, suppliers and customers with the idea of blackening their reputation with these people.

> Deliberately presenting facts in a misleading manner, plain lying, creating a false impression about your own interests. (e.g.: you are prepared to pay 4,000 euros for a study but tell everyone that 3,000 euros is your maximum.) Lying about factual matters (e.g., giving the wrong cost price figures) and offering worthless guarantees that you have no intention of keeping.

> Abusing the other person's trust. This includes the illegal gathering of information (for example through bribery or through infiltration of your negotiating partner's network).

> Bluffing. This involves making false promises or issuing empty threats: "If you do this, I can guarantee you a perfect service. If you do that, I will feel obliged to pass on this information to..." You know, of course, that you will never be able to provide a perfect service, nor will you ever be bothered to make that threatening report. But the idea that you might can sometimes work in your favour.

Let's return briefly to Ben & Jerry's's versus Häagen-Dazs. Few people will dispute that Ben & Jerry's's has a reputation for high moral standards. Even so, in our case study you can see that they were prepared to use the second of the above tactics without a moment's hesitation. They took matters to a higher level, involved the Pillsbury holding and launched an attack on the poor, innocent doughboy! This shows equally that neither Häagen-Dazs nor Ben & Jerry's's had a real problem with the first tactic: they were both prepared to fight tooth and nail to defend their own interests.

Other research carried out in America has shown that a group of priests found all five of the above tactics to be unacceptable, whereas a group of MBA students found all five to be perfectly reasonable. This does not mean, of course, that all MBA students are bandits! It should be remembered that the students were often assessing case studies with a short-term perspective for which there was no shadow of the future. And in these circumstances, it seems that they were prepared to consider most things, if it helped them to get their own way.

This is a relevant point. The best encouragement to making honest agreements is the prospect of having to make other agreements with the same negotiating partners at some point in the future. The more transient or unique a transaction is, the more likely we are to be economical with the truth. You won't be dealing with these dummies again – so why worry about your reputation? One-off negotiations with unknown parties are a recipe for trouble – just ask any negotiator who has experience of working abroad.

WATCH YOUR WORDS...

Julia Minson (Wharton Business School) and two of her colleagues asked themselves whether the manner of asking questions has any effect on concessions in negotiating situations.[64] The starting point for their study was simple but brilliant. Negotiation literature constantly repeats the following assertion: whoever asks a question gains information; whoever answers a question gives away information. This implies that you should be quick to ask questions – and slow to answer them. But Minson and her team commented shrewdly that you also give away lots of information by the nature of the questions you ask! What questions do you repeat? Which themes keep cropping up? How hard do you push for an answer? Perhaps even more importantly: is the answer actually dependent on the manner in which you pose the question?

The researchers allowed students to negotiate online for the sale of a second-hand iPod. All the students were sellers. The buyer was a research assistant, working to a fixed script. There were serious technical problems with the iPod, which might recur at any moment. At the start, one third of the sellers (condition 1) received a (computer-generated) general question: "What can you tell me about the iPod?" Another third (condition 2) received the question: "Is everything in order with the iPod?" The remaining third (condition 3) received the question: "What problems have you had with this iPod?" The answers given by the sellers varied tremendously, depending on the way in which the question was asked. If the buyer didn't ask about problems, he wouldn't be told about problems. In response to the general question (condition 1) only 10% of the sellers were 'honest' in their answer. When asked if everything was in order (condition 2), the level of honesty rose to 59%. When asked openly what was wrong (condition 3), no fewer than 87% preferred not to lie. In other words, the most direct question was also the most efficient – from the buyer's point of view. It is interesting to note that this was not a matter of ethics. After all, in answer to the third question only 13% chose to lie – the proverbial 'rotten apples'. But in answer to the first general question we must remember that a staggering 90% chose not to tell the truth. It is therefore apparently regarded as normal not to tell a buyer about potential problems unless he specifically asks.

As we (and the Romans) said earlier: *Caveat emptor*! This was clearly confirmed by further research. In a second study students were allowed to read answers given by real salespeople that in essence were identical to the misleading answers given to the three questions during the first study. They were asked to assess who was actually responsible for the fact that the truth failed to come out? Remarkably enough, it was now the buyer who was held to be jointly responsible for his failure to properly investigate the poor quality of the iPod! For conditions 1 and 2, there was little sympathy for the poor old *emptor*. Only under condition 3, where the salesperson was blatantly lying, was the seller identified as being exclusively responsible for the truth remaining hidden. In other words, lying is okay, as long as lying means 'withholding tactical information'. Or to put it another way: ethics are dependent on context and interpretation. Forgetting to say something is clearly a lesser offense than telling deliberate falsehoods.

So remember: the next time you buy a car or a computer, don't forget to ask: "What kind of problems am I likely to have?" Don't ask questions that are designed to make you feel reassured ("This won't shrink, will it?", "Apple computers don't get viruses, do they?"). Life really is like a restaurant: you usually get what you ask for. Just make sure to ask the right things in the right way!

THE USE OF EMOTIONS

When people communicate with each other, they use words and arguments. But they also use feelings and emotions. Their body language is the carrier of these emotions and as everyone now knows, body language has a far greater impact than spoken language. This is no different in negotiating situations. The idea that a poker face is the ideal pose for a negotiator is no longer true. You only need to watch the World Series of Poker for five minutes on television to see how today's modern professionals play the game. They bombard their opponents with a constant stream of emotions, some of which may be misleading – or not.

This is perfectly normal. There is nothing 'grey' or 'black' about the use of emotions during negotiations. On the contrary, negotiations without emotions are false and unreal. People always have emotions. So emotionless negotiations imply that everybody is hiding something. And just as the deliberate withholding of factual information is 'grey', so the suppression of your emotions is also 'grey'.

Nothing is more stupid than to make a threat that you know you are never going to carry out. Sometimes, people use intense emotion to try and underline to the other side that they are 'serious' ("My God, he really means it!"). But deliberately stage-managed emotions which are only intended to lend credibility to spurious threats are usually regarded as 'black'. It is simply lying: not about facts, but about emotions.

HOW TO RESPOND TO EMOTIONAL OUTBURSTS

You should treat emotional outbursts like any other form of communication. To respond to them rationally, you need to remain as analytical as possible. Try to separate the content of the message from the relational aspects. If you do this, you will soon notice that most emotional outbursts have little to do with the substance of the negotiations, but are more about you. *You* are too slow, *you* are lacking in goodwill, *you* are too stupid to understand what is in your own best interests. Try to respond as neutrally as possible to this kind of accusation and make maximum use of the EPS method when communication becomes really difficult.

Always begin with the E of Empathy: "I can see that you have a problem with the pace of our discussions", "I'm afraid that I underestimated just how important the delivery date is for you", "Yes, you are right: in this way we are indeed in danger of not reaching an agreement by the weekend".

Follow this up by remaining as upbeat as you can with the P for Positive: "Rest assured, we will look for a suitable solution as quickly as possible", "Yes, it has all been a bit slow, but as soon as we agree a delivery date things will pick up speed", "Have no fears: my team and I want nothing more than to collaborate successfully with your organization".

Only then should you move on to the S for Solution. "Consequently, we suggest a re-examination of the different elements of the cost price, one by one", "Let's waste no more time but do everything we can to reduce the delivery period to a minimum", "We are thinking in concrete terms of a timescale of at least three years".

THE FIVE STEPS OF PSYCHOLOGICAL MANIPULATION

A good relationship between the parties is a negotiating condition, but not an objective in itself. With psychological manipulation, matters are turned on their head. The relationship is the name of the game. Every negotiator – and that includes you – should know the rules of this game, in case they are used against you.

Step 1: Build a relationship

The first step seems a fairly obvious one. And it is something that the manipulator excels in. Observing his 'victim' closely is his trademark. Once he has all the information he needs, he moves in and seeks first contact. His aim is to 'press all the right buttons'. The super-manipulators (even manipulators have their pecking order) provide 'bait': a temptation to attract their prey. We know intuitively that someone who speaks to us out of the blue is often after something. For this reason, it is better that the victim should first approach his hunter. The art of seduction in the field of negotiation is largely unexplored territory. But you can reasonably assume that 80% of all marketing communication is designed to tempt the target, in the hope that *he* will enter into negotiations with a salesperson. In other words, the manipulator must make the first step as easy, pleasant and cheap as possible. Useful possibilities include samples, test subscriptions, free membership, a disarming smile...

Step 2: Make the relationship seem attractive

The second step is also one that we all recognize. We are overwhelmed with compliments. We get lots of nice presents and plenty of flattering attention. We are promised all kinds of wonderful things and some of those promises are actually kept. As a result, we may even become addicted to the relationship. The other party is just so interesting and appealing! Our other relationships are all more boring, difficult, anonymous... Typical moves in Step 2 include: "You are unique", "You are attractive" (intellectually, physically, psychologically), "You are a desirable proposition – who wouldn't want to do business with you?", "Unlike most of my clients, you have the capital to make a difference", "Your success is no fluke".

Step 3: Exchange the relationship for a minor interest

So far, nothing unusual has happened. The first two steps are a bit like being in love. You just want to do your best for the other person. Or so it seems. We all know that at the end of the day the manipulator does not have his victim's best interests at heart. He has his own interests at heart. Gradually, the victim becomes aware, sometimes subtly, sometimes directly, that all the presents, compliments and friendliness have an ulterior motive, that some kind of favour in return is required. Typical moves in Step 3 include: "Can I ask you something personal?", "I hardly like to ask, but would you mind...", "I wouldn't ask just anyone, but you are different...", "This needs to be kept between the two of us, but I have a unique opportunity for you..."

Step 4: Raise the stakes

Little by little, the victim is asked to do more and more. And once you have made the first small commitment, it is difficult to pull back. After the victim has been hooked into a friendly relationship, he is now told that the relationship might not remain quite so friendly, unless he is compliant. In fact, it might become positively unfriendly, if he fails to do what he is asked. The tone becomes dictatorial and commandeering. We are now in the realms of emotional blackmail.

Typical moves in Step 4 include: "Surely you aren't going to leave me in the lurch?", "How can you desert me after all that I have invested in our relationship?", "I have just one more thing to ask, but it is a crucial test for our collaboration", "There are very few people I would share this with, because it is risky, not something for wimps – but if you agree, you'll never regret it".

Step 5: Aftercare

After the victim has been bled dry, the manipulator will do all he can to convince him that he has actually done him a big favour! This is not only intended to keep the victim sweet, but also to prepare him for a next possible sting.

Typical moves in Step 5 include: "That was a unique collaboration; what a pity that luck was against us", "I am really sorry that things didn't work out, but who could have predicted that...", "I have never worked with someone who is so open and creative – it was a real privilege and I hope that you can also look back on our collaboration with some satisfaction – let's hope it goes better next time...'

HOW CAN YOU COUNTERACT PSYCHOLOGICAL MANIPULATION?

If you look closely at the five-step analysis of psychological manipulation, it should be clear that at each step you can avoid lending a helping hand to your own downfall. The sooner you react in an appropriate way, the easier it becomes to escape. Whatever you do, you must ensure that you never allow step 3 to be implemented against you. That is the point of no return. To prevent this from happening, you can use the following tactics:

- Step 1. Don't let the relationship start: avoid eye-contact, fob the manipulator off with an excuse, move on to talk to somebody else. In an organizational context, the best method is to refer to a general rule ("Sorry, but the policy of our company is...", "We never talk about...", "We are not allowed to accept...").
- *Step 2.* Remember that we are all susceptible to compliments – including you! If you say that you hate compliments, the manipula-

tor might reply: "Yes, I can see that you are someone who prefers to decide things for himself." In these circumstances, fewer than 10% of people realize that they are still being flattered. We all like to have our identity confirmed by others. Even seemingly non-relevant comments can work in a similar way. A nice remark about your car, your garden, your clothes, your approach, your results, your children... We all love to hear these things. The best way to deal with flattery and excessive attention is to turn it on the user. In this way, you are making your own preparations for Step 3: "If you think I'm so good, it's probably going to cost you a fortune!" Humour is probably the best weapon ("I bet you say that to all the boys!"). Exaggerating the compliment still further also works well ("Yeah, you're right, I'm unique. I'll probably win the Nobel Prize next year").

> *Step 3*. This is the most critical step. Here the rule is clear. NEVER take this step. Simply refuse. Do not exchange relational benefits for your basic interests – unless, of course, you are willing to be manipulated ("Daddy, you're the sweetest man in all the world"). But in all other cases: STOP! Make clear to the manipulator that you understand what he is proposing and then reject the offer out of hand. Because if you reach Step 4, it's already too late.

With good insights into the ethical sensitivities of negotiations, you know that...

... the ethical sensitivities of the situation are largely dependent on the way in which you FRAME the negotiations. If you regard the negotiations as a battle that you must win at all costs, there is a good chance that you will find most things acceptable. Some negotiators are still happy to use 'white' and 'grey' tricks. If the negotiations are regarded as an anonymous, one-off event with no future perspective, tactics such as fighting exclusively for your own interests, providing misleading information about your own position and concealing your BATNA are also generally accepted. On the other hand, if you see negotiation as a 'win-win' process, you will understand that negotiations have a past and, above all, a future. You will also realize that by systematically applying the lessons of this book you should usually be able to avoid the need for 'white lies'. At the same time, you remain aware that some unscrupulous negotiators are prepared to push matters to the extreme. They are willing to lie blatantly and to destabilize their negotiating partners, thereby overstepping the boundaries of ethical decency. These 'black' dirty tricks can do great pain and harm, but are not sustainable in the long-term. The 'smart' negotiator KNOWS how the manipulators work but REFUSES to use their tactics. He will make sure that he does not lend a 'friendly hand' to his own downfall. He is not the idiot in the room.

Here is a final summary of the most frequently used dirty tricks and the best way to react to them:

BLACK OR DARK-GREY TRICKS USED BY THE OTHER PARTY	CONSTRUCTIVE REACTION
› CREATING EMOTIONAL TENSION THROUGH LONG DELAYS, SMALL IRRITATIONS, ETC.	› RELAX, MAKE SURE YOU HAVE PLENTY OF TIME, TELL EVERYONE THAT YOU ARE RENOWNED FOR YOUR GREAT PATIENCE, EXPLAIN THAT DURING THE DELAY YOU WERE ABLE TO DO PLENTY OF OTHER INTERESTING THINGS, THANK THE OTHER PARTY FOR THIS EXTRA TIME.
› EMOTIONAL OUTBURSTS	› CALMLY REFLECT THE EMOTIONS ("I CAN SEE NOW THAT THIS IS REALLY VERY IMPORTANT FOR YOU").
› ATTEMPTS AT DESTABILIZATION (FOR EXAMPLE, TRYING TO GET YOU DRUNK)	› AVOID THE FIRST GLASS, APPEAL TO A 'HIGHER PRINCIPLE' (E.G. RELIGIOUS BELIEFS, HEALTH).
› ATTEMPTS AT DESTABILIZATION (FOR EXAMPLE, AN EMOTIONAL PERSONAL ATTACK)	› SAY WHAT YOU HEAR AND PLAY IT BACK ("YOU ARE BEING VERY PERSONAL", "HOW CAN YOU BE SO SURE OF MY INTENTIONS?").
› YOU THINK THAT THE OTHER PARTY WILL LIE	› AGREE FROM THE START THAT ALL FACTS AND FIGURES CAN BE CHECKED BY BOTH PARTIES.
› GOOD COP/BAD COP	› SAY WHAT YOU SEE: "YOU TWO SEEM TO HAVE A VERY DIFFERENT VIEW OF THE NEGOTIATIONS".
› PSYCHOLOGICAL MANIPULATION	› NEVER EXCHANGE INTERESTS FOR GOOD RELATIONS; EXCHANGE INTERESTS FOR INTERESTS.

ENDNOTES

1. Some studies conclude that managers spend as much as 42% of their time resolving conflicts. See: Watson, C. & Hoffman, L.R. (1996). Managers as negotiators: A test of power versus gender as predictors of feelings, behavior and outcomes. The *Leadership Quarterly*, 7(1), 63-85.
2. See, for example, the article: 'Five tips to successfully retain generation Y managers.' Retrieved 1 June 2011, from whatdoyouwantfromthem.blogspot.com.
3. Karras, C.L. (1996). *In business as in life, you don't get what you deserve, you get what you negotiate.* Los Angeles: Stanford Street Press.
4. This quote comes from: De Waal, F. (2009). *The age of empathy. Nature's lessons for a kinder society.* New York: Crown.
5. Darwin distanced himself from some of the interpretations Spencer gave to his work.
6. This is a remark by Andrew Carnegie, a Scottish-born American industrialist and philanthropist (1835-1919).
7. James, W. (1890). *The principles of psychology*, vol. II. New York: Dover Publications, page 412. William James (1842-1910) was an American philosopher and psychologist, leader of the philosophical movement of pragmatism.
8. Reilly, P. (2009). Was Machiavelli right? Lying in negotiation and the art of defensive self-help. *Ohio State Journal on Dispute Resolution*, 24, 481-533. Reilly raised the question of whether lying and deception are actually advantageous for negotiation results.
9. Slaikeu, K.A. & Hasson, R.H. (1998). *Controlling the costs of conflict. How to design a system for your organization.* San Francisco: Jossey-Bass.
10. CPP (2008). A study of 5,000 people in nine countries in the EU, the US and South Africa. 'Workplace conflict and how business can harness it to thrive.' Retrieved 1 June 2011, from https://www.cpp.com/pdfs/CPP_Global_Human_Capital_Report_Workplace_Conflict.pdf
11. International Law Firm Fulbright & Jaworkski LLP (2005). 'Litigation trends survey.' Retrieved 1 June 2011, from http://www.fulbright.com/index.cfm?fuseaction=correspondence.formfindings. The survey was carried out in the US but a similar trend is evident in Europe.

12. De Waal, F. (2005). *Our Inner Ape*. New York: Riverhead Books.

13. Our schedule is based on other different basic schedules available in the negotiation literature. The most well-known of these is Blake & Mouton, who quickly translated their managerial grid to the negotiating world. The most widely used is the Thomas-Kilmann Conflict Mode Instrument. The 'dual concern model' by Pruitt is also referred to frequently in the literature.

14. You build up your reputation on the basis of the negotiation pathway you have followed. In this way, each negotiation counts towards your negotiation CV. So be careful, even with one-off negotiations, because they can still damage your long-term reputation.

15. Goleman, D. (1996). *Emotional intelligence: why it can matter more than IQ*. New York: Bantam Books.

16. According to Saner two-thirds of the skills that you need to become a negotiator can be learned or trained: Saner, R. (1997). *The expert negotiator: strategy, tactics, motivation, behavior, leadership*. Leiden: Brill Academic.

17. This is a basic concept from: Fisher, R., Patton, B. & Ury, W. (1991). *Getting to yes. Negotiating an agreement without giving in*. New York: Penguin Group.

18. This story is most commonly attributed to Mary Parker Follett.

19. Ross, L.D. & Ward, A. (1996). 'Naive realism in everyday life: Implications for social conflict and misunderstanding.' In: Brown, T., Reed, E. & Turiel, E. (Eds.) *Values and knowledge* (pp. 103-135). Hillsdale, NJ: Lawrence Erlbaum Associates.

20. Martin, R.L. (2007). *The opposable mind. Winning through integrative thinking*. Boston: Harvard Business Press.

21. Barrett, F.J. & Fry, R.E. (2008). *Appreciative inquiry. A positive approach to building cooperative capacity*. Chagrin Falls, Ohio: The Taos Institute Publications; Watkins, J.M. & Mohr, B.J. (2001). *Appreciative inquiry. Change at the speed of imagination*. San Francisco: Jossey-Bass/Pfeiffer.

22. Lax, D.A. & Sebenius, J.K. (1986). *The manager as negotiator. Bargaining for cooperation and competitive gain*. New York: Free Press.

23. Byttebier, I. (2002). *Creativiteit. HOE? ZO! Inzicht, inspiratie en toepassingen voor het optimaal benutten van uw eigen creativiteit en die van uw organisatie*. Tielt: Lannoo.

24. Souter, N. (2007). *Breakthrough thinking. Brainstorming for inspiration and ideas*. New York: Sterling Publishing.

25. See Souter, op.cit.
26. THis table is based on various parallel publications from the so-called 'Harvard School'.
27. Martin, R.L. (2007). *The opposable mind. Winning through integrative thinking.* Boston: Harvard Business Press.
28. Thompson, L.L. (2008). *The truth about negotiations.* Upper Saddle River, NJ: FT Press, page 91
29. See for example: Malhotra, D. & Bazerman, M.H. (2007). *Negotiation genius: how to overcome obstacles and achieve brilliant results at the bargaining table and beyond.* Bantam Books: New York.
30. See for example: Craver, C.B. (2005). 'Aspirations, anchoring, and negotiation results.' *The Negotiator Magazine.* Retrieved 1 June 2011, from www.negotiatormagazine.com/craver_october2005.doc and Van Poucke, D., & Buelens, M. (2002). 'Predicting the outcome of a two-party price negotiation: Contribution of reservation price, aspiration price and opening offer.' *Journal of Economic Psychology, 23*(1), 67-76.
31. BAWA is better known in negotiating circles under the name BATNA: Best Alternative To Negotiated Agreement. BATNA was first launched in 1981 in the bestseller *Getting to Yes* by Roger Fisher and William Ury: Fisher, R., Patton, B. & Ury, W. (1991). *Getting to Yes. Negotiating an agreement without giving in.* New York: Penguin Group.
32. Buelens, M., & Van Poucke, D. (2004). 'Determinants of a negotiator's initial opening offer.' *Journal of Business and Psychology, 19*(1), 23-35.
33. Friedman, G. & Himmelstein, J. (2008). *Challenging conflict: mediation through understanding.* American Bar Association in cooperation with the Program on Negotiation at Harvard Law School.
34. Huguenin, P. (2004). *Conflicthantering en onderhandelen. Effectief handelen bij conflicten en tegenstellingen.* Houten: Bohn Stafleu Van Loghum.
35. Fisher, R., Ury, W. & Patton, B. (2007). *Excellent onderhandelen. Een praktische gids voor het best mogelijke resultaat in elke onderhandeling.* Amsterdam: Business Contact.
36. Cialdini, R.B. (2001). *The power of persuasion*, DVD, Stanford Breakfast Briefings.
37. The name, prisoner's dilemma, was first used by Albert W. Tucker. There are literally hundreds of scientific publications about this game-theory game. It is

famous – or notorious – because there is no ideal outcome. It is almost as if you are doomed to lose with the other player.

38. There are several interesting studies on the theme of 'procedural fairness'. See for example: Lind, E.A. & Tyler, T.R. (1988). *The social psychology of procedural justice (critical issues in social justice)* Springer and Kim, W.C. & Mauborgne, R. (1997). 'Fair process: managing in the knowledge economy.' *Harvard Business Review, 75*(4), 65–75.
39. Cialdini, R.B. (2006). *Influence: the psychology of persuasion.* HarperCollins Publishers Inc.
40. Lax, D.A. & Sebenius, J.K. (2006). *3-D negotiation. Powerful tools to change the game in your most important deals.* Boston: Harvard Business Press.
41. Based on: Watkins, J.M. (2006). *Shaping the game. The new leader's guide to effective negotiating.* Boston: Harvard Business Press.
42. See Watkins, op.cit.
43. Huthwaite International/IACCM (2009). *Improving corporate negotiation performance. A benchmark study of the world's largest organisations.* Retrieved 1 June 2011, from http://www.negotiationlawblog.com/uploads/file/improving-corporate-negotiation-performance.pdf
44. De Man, A.P. (2006). *Alliantiebesturing. Samenwerking als precisie-instrument.* Assen: Van Gorcum.
45. 'The three elements that are required to accelerate capability building – dynamic specialization, connectivity, and leveraged capability building across institutional boundaries – are relevant not only to business enterprises, but to a broad array of political, social, and educational institutions.' In: Hagel III, J. & Brown, J.S. (2005). *The only sustainable edge. Why business strategy depends on productive friction and dynamic specialization.* Boston: Harvard Business Press, page 3.
46. A remark by Tony Hughes, CEO of Huthwaite International.
47. Liberman, V., Samuels, S.M. & Ross, L. (2004). 'The name of the game: predictive power of reputations versus situational labels in determining prisoner's dilemma game moves.' *Personality and Social Psychology Bulletin, 30*(9), 1175-1185.
48. Hardin, G. (1968). 'The tragedy of the commons.' *Science, 162*(3859), 1243-1248.
49. Ostrom, E. (2007). *Governing the commons: the evolution of institutions for collective action (political economy of institutions and decisions).* Cambridge: Cambridge University Press.

50. Benkler, Y. (2011). 'The unselfish gene.' *Harvard Business Review, 89*(7-8), 76-85.
51. Benkler, Y. (2011). *The penguin and the leviathan: how cooperation triumphs over self-interest.* New York: Crown Business.
52. Ertel, D. (1999). 'Turning negociation into a corporate capability.' *Harvard Business Review*, 77 (3), 55-68.
53. See: Movius, H. & Susskind, L. (2009). *Built to win. Creating a world-class negotiating organization.* Boston: Harvard Business School Press; Ertel, D. (1999). 'Turning negotiation into a corporate capability.' *Harvard Business Review*, 77(3), 55-70; Ertel, D. & Gordon, M. (2007). *The point of the deal. How to negotiate when 'yes' is not enough.* Boston: Harvard Business School Press.
54. Wiesenfeld, B.M., Rothman, N.B., Wheeler-Smith S.L. & Galinsky, A.D. (2011). 'Why fair bosses fall behind.' *Harvard Business Review, 89*(7-8), 26.
55. Benkler, Y. (2011). *The penguin and the leviathan: how cooperation triumphs over self-interest.* New York: Crown Business.
56. Huthwaite International/IACCM (2009). *Improving corporate negotiation performance. A benchmark study of the world's largest organisations.* Retrieved 1 June 2011, from http://www.negotiationlawblog.com/uploads/file/improving-corporate-negotiation-performance.pdf
57. Movius, H. & Susskind, L. (2009). *Built to win. Creating a world-class negotiating organization.* Boston: Harvard Business School Press
58. Dozens of books and articles have been written to map out the different cognitive biases, also in the field of negotiation. For a good summary of the most relevant 'mental misleaders', see: Buelens, M., & Van Poucke, D. (2001). 'De cognitieve benadering van het onderhandelingsproces.' *Sociaal en Economisch Tijdschrift*, 55(4), 591-617.
59. See for example: Sadler-Smith, E.(2008). *Inside intuition.* Abingdon: Routledge.
60. Curhan, J. R., & Pentland, A. (2007). 'Thin slices of negotiation: Predicting outcomes from conversational dynamics within the first 5 minutes.' *Journal of Applied Psychology, 92*(3), 802-811.
61. For the factual details of this case, see: www.letmewatchthis.ch/watch-572255-Blood-on-the-Carpet-Ice cream-Wars).
62. There is quite a good book about 'negotiating with the devil': Mnookin, R. (2010). *Bargaining with the devil: when to negotiate, when to fight.* New York: Simon & Schuster.

63. In addition to Robinson and his colleagues, there are several other interesting studies that explore the ethical behaviour of negotiators: Robinson, R.J., Lewicki, R.J., & Donahue, E.M. (2000). 'Extending and testing a five factor model of ethical and unethical bargaining tactics: introducing the SINS scale.' *Journal of Organizational Behavior, 21*(6), 649-664; Lewicki, R.J., & Robinson, R.J. (1998). 'Ethical and unethical bargaining tactics: An empirical study.' *Journal of Business Ethics, 17*(6), 665-682; Schweitzer, M.E., DeChurch, L.A., & Gibson, D.E. (2005). 'Conflict frames and the use of deception: Are competitive negotiators less ethical?' *Journal of Applied Social Psychology, 35*(10), 2123-2149; Volkema, R., Fleck, D., & Hofmeister, A. (2010). 'Predicting Competitive-Unethical Negotiating Behavior and Its Consequences.' *Negotiation Journal, 26*(3), 263-286; Cohen, T.R. (2010). 'Moral Emotions and Unethical Bargaining: The differential effects of empathy and perspective taking in Ddeterring deceitful negotiation.' *Journal of Business Ethics, 94*(4), 569-579.

64. Minson, J., Ruedi, N., & Schweitzer, M.E. (2011). *Ask (the right way) and you shall receive: the effect of question type on disclosure and deception.* Paper presented at the Academy of Management Conference, San Antonio.

ABOUT THE SERIES AND THE AUTHORS

With *Essentials* you can become a successful manager in the twinkling of an eye – or the turning of a page. In seven useful, easy-to-use books you can learn everything you need to know about the current themes that no modern manager can afford to ignore. The series is written by authors from the Vlerick Business School. Each book is based on the very latest scientific research, supplemented with useful practical tips and advice.

Prof. Dr. Katia Tieleman has 15 years of experience as a top negotiator and negotiating adviser for various major companies and international organisations (UNO, OECD, EU, the World Bank). She is partner-professor of Negotiation and Conflict Management at the Vlerick Business School and is attached to the Harvard Program on Negotiation at the Harvard Law School. Worldwide, she has trained thousands of top executives, experts, MBA and Master students. [She currently has two other books in preparation.]

Prof. Dr. Marc Buelens lectures in management and is a partner-professor of the Vlerick Business School. He is a weekly columnist in *Trends* magazine and has published several books on management. Together with his wife, Ann Vermeiren, he wrote a bestseller on self-care (*Beter Zorgen voor Jezelf*). His many articles on negotiation have appeared in leading magazines of international repute.

FURTHER INFORMATION

Prof. dr. Katia Tieleman combines excellent research and teaching with 15 years of experience as a consultant and top level negotiator. Out of the cross-fertilisation of these activities arose the NQ® concept that was launched with this book.

Katia Tieleman also works on the development of a scan for NQ® and Corporate NQ®, which helps negotiators and companies to measure and optimise their negotiating intelligence, as such improving their bottom and top lines.

She heads an Centre at the Vlerick Business School where she translates NQ® into practice, together with a number of corporate front runners.

Katia Tieleman trains executives in NQ® negotiating, influencing and conflict management.

To find out more about the new negotiating intelligence paradigm NQ® and Corporate NQ®, or about training programmes and other initiatives, please contact: katia.tieleman@vlerick.com